THE LONDON, TILBURY & SOUTHEND RAILWAY

A History of the Company and Line

by

PETER KAY

Volume One: 1836 - 1893

For all Southend commuters who ever wondered why they are there.

The men of the LT&SR. This view comes unidentified but it can be located as Southend, with the photographer standing by the Platform 1 bay line and facing north. Clearly there is some building work going on, and it may be 1899 when the goods yard on the north side was greatly enlarged and a new goods shed built; such a date would seem about right generally. The photograph was clearly not officially inspired as the Stationmaster has not graced the scene with his presence.

Ken Nunn Collection LCGB (photo by H.L. Hopwood)

INTRODUCTION
AND ACKNOWLEDGEMENTS

The London Tilbury & Southend line has attracted a fair attention already in recent decades. A good short Oakwood history of the company by H. D. Welch appeared as far back as 1951, after which it was not until 1981 that George Dow's *London Tilbury & Southend Album* added greatly to the photographic coverage of the line in print. On the locomotive front, C. Langley Aldrich's 1945 book was effectively superseded by Kenneth Leech's *Loco Profile 27:Tilbury Tanks* in 1972; loco sheds were then covered by Hawkins & Reeve in *LMS Engine Sheds Vol 4* (WSP, 1984) and wagons by Bob Essery in *An Illustrated History of Midland Wagons Vol 2* (OPC, 1980). Very recently, R.W. Rush's *Locomotives and Rolling Stock of the London Tilbury & Southend Railway* (Oakwood, 1994) has covered coaches for the first time. Ken Frost's *The Romford-Upminster Branch* of 1964 has been the only book on a particular section of the system; this branch has also been covered by several magazine articles, a reflection more of its separability than its importance!

Despite these specialist works, there has up to now still been nothing to expand on Welch's work as an overall history of the company and the line. This book is the first in a two-volume history initiated in the belief that the time had come for such a more detailed account. Within it will be found a full history of the LT&SR company up to 1893, plus a number of features on particular locations or train services. The second volume will take the story on to 1912. With the LT&SR being a relatively small company it is possible to cover the development of local infrastructural details here in a manner not practicable in the history of a large company (albeit not in the same depth as one might now be expected to do in a work on a minor branch line). It is also hoped to produce, in the fullness of time, further works or articles covering in depth certain other locations not featured in these volumes for lack of space. The reservation of material for these inevitably involves a certain lack of 'balance' here; those interested in places not included here must, unfortunately, exercise patience until their time comes.

The Tottenham & Forest Gate and Whitechapel & Bow joint lines will be covered (in Volume 2) insofar as their promotion and construction, and interrelationship with the LT&S line, are concerned; there is also a 'feature' on the St Pancras - Southend services. However, the T&FG was effectively part of the Midland system from opening, as that company maintained the line and provided the main train services; and the W&B similarly became effectively part of the District. Full coverage of the stations and local train services on these lines would therefore be inappropriate in a book on the LT&SR, and has not been attempted here. Again, the Fenchurch Street - Gas Factory Junction section, much as we have in BR days come to think of it as part of the 'LT&S', was of course a GER line of which the pre-1912 LT&SR was only a minority user; its history is therefore outside the scope of this work except insofar as the limitations of its infrastructure affected LT&SR train services and thereby indeed the whole fate of the LT&SR company itself.

This book makes no attempt, either, to cover the details of LT&SR locomotives, coaches and wagons, which have all been dealt with already in the works referred to above (amongst the locomotive histories, Leech's is to be preferred). More could of course still be said on the fine details, but this general history of the line is not the place for such technicalities.

The research for this book has (as ever) been carried out primarily at the Public Record Office, Kew; also at the Essex County Record Offices (Chelmsford and Southend), the Greater London Record Office, the House of Lords Record Office, the British Library (British Museum and Holborn), the PLA Library, the Railway Studies Library, Newton Abbot, the Reference Libraries at Grays and Gravesend, and Valence House Museum and Library Becontree. Inevitably I have also received much help from many other people. In the pleasant task of thanking them, I must begin by mentioning those who have made available the results of their own researches. John Gough had already collected a large amount of material on the LT&S line in connection with his book *The Midland Railway:A Chronology,* and this saved me from having to deal with some sources myself; we have also had a detailed correspondence attempting to make sense of some of the more difficult evidence in the available sources. Some of the information received originated from Roger Newman's researches into Midland signalling. Paul Armstrong has supplied a large amount of information from his collection of BR period notices for the LT&S line, and also consulted several of his fellow signalmen for their recollections of the working of the line in pre-electrification days. John Ormston, whose book *The Five Minute Crossing* on the Tilbury-Gravesend ferry first came to my notice on that sad day in November 1992 when Tilbury Riverside closed, has proved a most helpful correspondent.. H.D. Welch, of whose present day whereabouts I had no idea, appeared 'out of the blue' when he contacted the Newton Abbot Railway Studies Library to deposit his LT&SR research notes there; I was able to make use of them, so this book can in some way claim to be a true child of its 1951 predecessor. Charles Phillips of the LT&SR Society offered numerous suggestions, as did John Watling and others in the Great Eastern Railway Society. Edwin Course assisted with both personal recollection and research knowledge. Tony Nelson made available his bibliography of published LT&SR material. Mrs Frances Dunbar let me see what was left of the late Andrew Ivor Dunbar's collection. Bill Hearn and Jack Whittington helped with their memories of the line in the LMS period and the irreplaceable Kenneth Leech with recollections of the real LT&SR (a mere 82 years after its passing!). Richard Foster, Reg Instone and John Talbot assisted with information on signalling matters. Of those who are no longer with us, Ken Nunn, H.V. Borley and T.S. Lascelles left correspondence and notes, in the Welch files and at Brunel University, which have helped with the project. Much of all the above will only appear in the subsequent volumes rather than here.

For photographs I am particularly grateful to Dave Taylor, Dick Riley, Richard Casserley, Peter Paton, Bruce Ellis, Gordon Hales, Peter Snell (Frank Church collection), Graham Stacey (LCGB Ken Nunn collection), Ken Cook, and others as per acknowledgements. Unfortunately the LT&S line was hardly photographed at all prior to 1900 (a fact that has naturally brought difficulties in illustrating this first volume in particular) and most of the active photographers in the Edwardian years restricted themselves to locomotive portraits, so that the supply of unpublished pre-1912 photographs of use is now beginning to run very low. Sometimes one has to use previously-published views because their full value has not been taken advantage of in previous captioning, but on the whole I have tried to avoid repeating well-known views, in particular those in the Dow album which most readers will already have on their shelves (references are given to photographs in this album where they are useful in illustrating points being made here).

Thanks also to Glenys Brownhill for her patience in complicated typing corrections and to Offset Graphics for putting the book together quickly at short notice.

The LT&S line has never attracted those who seek scenery and grand expresses. It has long simply got on with its job of being a serious railway, piling it high and selling it cheap. It changed the area through which it passed more than almost any other railway in the country. Not for nothing was it described in the 1840s as a line 'from Ilford to the World's End'. Today the World's End is one of the few places in the area that an 1840s visitor might still recognise, for every station on the line (bar Low Street) has generated largescale housing development, heavy industry has sprawled, and the fields that stretched for miles of marshland silence are now shrunk to brief and unsatisfactory interludes between merging towns. Margate, Clacton, Melbourne and Bombay may no longer appear on the LT&S departure boards as they once did, but Southend, the LT&SR's child, remains ever dependent on its railway.

Peter Kay
Teignmouth

17.xii.1994/28.vii.1996

The **London Tilbury & Southend Railway Society** exists to foster the study of the line. Contact the Secretary Charles Phillips, 52 Brookmans Road, Stock, Ingatestone, Essex CM4 9DB.

The **Great Eastern Railway Society** also covers all railways in South Essex. Contact the Membership Secretary J. Tant, 9 Clare Road, Leytonstone, London E11 1JU.

CONTENTS

An Index (to Volumes 1 and 2), and a note on sources, will appear in Volume 2.

CHAPTER 1

Rival Schemes (1836-1851)

SOUTH ESSEX IN 1840

Despite its closeness to the burgeoning city of London, the Thames-side Essex of pre-railway days was as remote an area as anywhere in Southern England. To the north the busy 'Essex Great Road' from London to Colchester served the long-established towns of Romford, Brentwood and Chelmsford; but Thames-side Essex was on the road to nowhere, little-populated and unvisited by outsiders. To the south, the river Thames itself was one of the world's busiest commercial waterways; but Essex men had little to do with the longer-distance shipping traffic, although the river was used for local transport to and from London via the wharves at Barking, Purfleet, Grays and various locations up the many creeks.

London stopped at the River Lea, and the area that was soon to become Canning Town and the Royal Docks was quiet marshland without habitation. East Ham was a straggling village in deep countryside, although the influence of London had made itself felt on the local economy insofar as the farms of East Ham, Little Ilford and Barking were largely given over to market gardening for the London market.

Barking was the one place in Thames-side Essex that might justifiably claim the outsider's attention. Famous in Saxon and mediaeval times for its wealthy abbey founded under St Etheldreda in 666, its prosperity had by the late eighteenth century became linked instead to its role as the home of the country's largest fishing fleet. By the 1840s there were some 180 smacks employing 1500 hands, almost all of whom lived in the town. The fleet was, however, run under a system by which the boats and men stayed out in the North Sea fishing grounds for lengthy periods, only returning home for occasional rest. The fish were never seen in Barking at all, as they were taken direct from the fishing grounds to Billingsgate by a special fleet of fast cutters.

Eastwards from Barking there lay only mile after mile of riverside marshes with quiet farming country behind. The only industrial activity was at Purfleet and Grays Thurrock (the only settlements actually on the river on the Essex side), where there were chalkpits with tramways running down to the river wharves. None of the inland villages was of any great size and few had potential for 'residential' purposes.

Only when the river met the sea, at Leigh and Southend, did one once again meet with non-agricultural activity. Leigh was an old-established fishing centre (although quite different from Barking in that the fishing, at this date mainly oysters for the London market, was all done locally). Finally the 'watering place' of Southend, served by London steamers calling at its lengthy pier, was still a small place as yet, although it had obvious prospects as the nearest seaside resort to London.

South Essex as it stood therefore offered precious little attraction to the railway promoter. As a way of getting to Kent, however, it had much in its favour. The very easy flat country, much easier than that on the Kent side, offered the prospect of very cheap railway construction which, in combination with the

The fons et origo of the London Tilbury & Southend - pleasure trippers arriving at Gravesend by steamboats from London Bridge. The Town Pier is seen in its original open form as built in 1834.

The industrial face of 20th-century Gravesend belies the fact that it was London's favourite daytrip destination in the period between the growth of steamboat services in the 1820s, and the 1840s/50s when the completion of railways to the Sussex and Kent seaside resorts started enabling Londoners to go further afield for the day. The first purpose-built attraction at Gravesend was the 'Terrace Gardens' just east of the town centre, opened in 1835 (with their own pier, the Terrace Pier), but they were soon eclipsed by the 'Rosherville Gardens' to the west of the town, opened by George Jones in 1837 originally with high ideas of botanical education but very quickly adapted for the mass pleasure market with sideshows, illuminations, a variety theatre and 'banqueting hall'. Rosherville too acquired its own private pier, opened in 1840.

Thanks to these additional attractions, the number of steamboat passengers at Gravesend increased from 290,420 in the year 1832/3 to 1,043,669 in 1840/1, most of this traffic being in the four-month summer season. The promoters of railways to Tilbury in the 1840s were naturally inclined to foresee this boom lasting forever! In the event, by the time the LT&SR opened in 1854, the popularity of Gravesend was passing its peak, although it remained a reasonably popular daytrip destination until the 1890s.

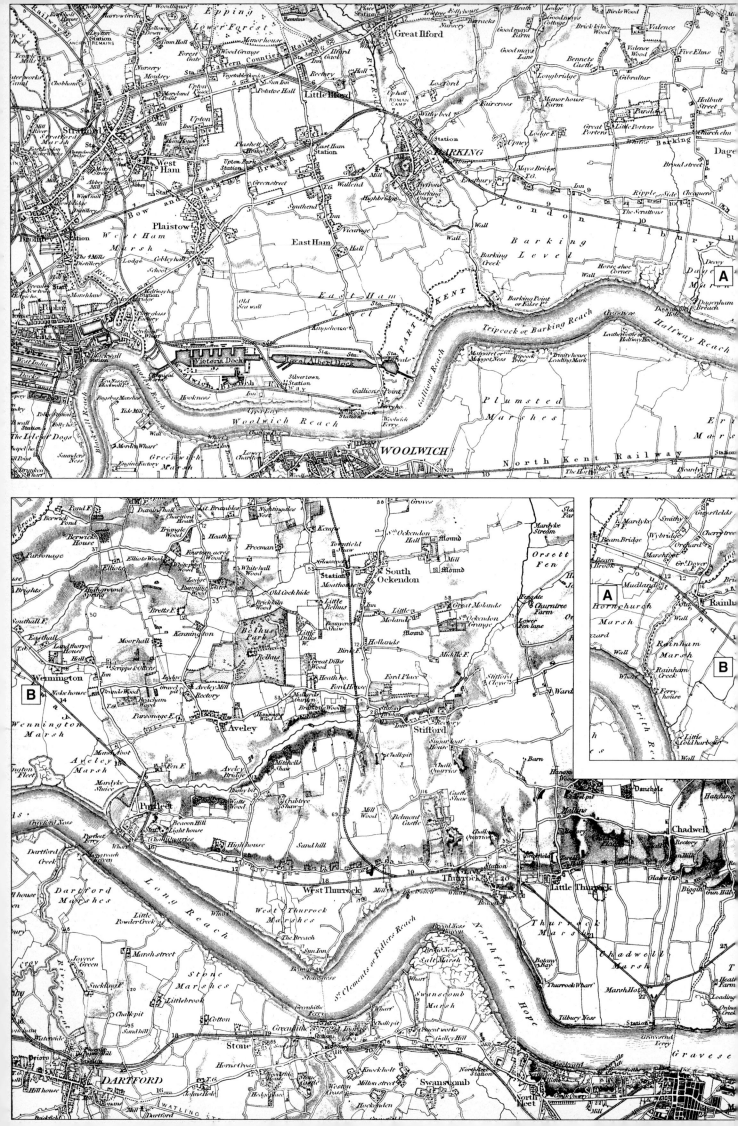

This 'Old Series' one inch map of Essex was first published in 1805, but was wholly revised in 1843/4 and thus gives a good picture of South Essex at the time of the railway promotions. There was no full revision after this but on this printing railways have been added to 1892 and certain other major developments added, particularly in London. Strictly speaking therefore, the map is a corrupt picture of mixed dates. In practice it is a valuable source.

Tilbury docks (1886) are not shown and indeed there has been no post-1840s revision of the Tilbury area at all; the Gravesend ferry is shown on its pre-railway route from Tilbury Fort (left as a 'white space' as a military secret on this printing) to Gravesend West Street. At Thames Haven the name 'Dock' appears, a very optimistic terminology for what was only a part-excavated hole at the time of the 1840s survey

and was destined never to proceed beyond that state. At Leigh there is a major error as the railway is shown on the 1852 Act line instead of on the line actually built, which makes one suspect that the OS were as a general policy adding railways from information seen on plans rather than from their own surveys. As the plates were frequently altered to accommodate other new railways, it seems odd that this error was not corrected.

The Crow Stone east of Leigh (later to give its name to an LT&SR loco) marked the limit of the jurisdiction of the Lord Mayor of London as Conservator of the River Thames.

Southend Pier had been built in 1830 in hopes of encouraging the steamboat companies who were neglecting Southend in favour of the Thanet resorts, which had convenient calling places in contrast to Southend's infamous mud-

flats (which prevented calls at low tide). Nevertheless it was to take some years to wean day-trippers towards Southend in really large numbers, and longer still before Southend began to grow significantly for residential purposes. In the 1840s Southend, as depicted here, still consisted of nothing but the High Street, the Royal Terrace, and half a mile of development along the front eastward from the pier.

This may be an appropriate place to mention the subsequent history of the pier, which many at one time thought belonged to the LT&SR. This it never did but it was owned by the GER and leased to Peto Brassey & Betts, so putting it in a rather similar position to the LT&S line itself.

The original pier company was forced to mortgage the pier to the Public Works Commissioners who put it up for auction in

continued over

August 1846. This coincided with the gestation of the ECR's Southend line scheme and the ECR therefore decided to buy the pier, partly one suspects because it might enable them to strangle the steamboat companies by inflating the pier landing tolls. The purchase was carried through in 1847 for £17,000 and the pier vested in the ownership of David Waddington the ECR Vice-Chairman 'under a declaration of trust in favour of the ECR'. It was let to a Mr.Bolton until 1854 and the ECR ownership did not become publicly noticeable. In the 1852 LT&SER Bill powers were sought to transfer the pier to the LT&SER undertaking, but this was struck out. Instead Peto

Brassey & Betts made an agreement with Waddington in August 1854 under which they leased the pier (from the end of Bolton's lease) at £1,000 a year, on the understanding that they would purchase it shortly for £20,000. The lease was to continue until 1871, but the purchase was evaded; and with Waddington's death, and then Peto and Betts' bankruptcy, most of those who understood the rather complex situation left the scene. In 1867 there were questions from the Inland Revenue and the GER officers had to try to get to the bottom of it, but it took three years legal work to get the formal ownership of the pier transferred from Waddington's infant heir-at-law

to the GER company itself, so that it could then be sold to Brassey. No sooner was this done than Brassey died and the eventual sale in April 1871 was to Brassey's trustees. They in turn sold the pier to the Southend Local Board in 1875 for a mere £12,000, and the 'railway' connection ceased.

The new iron pier, replacing the 1830 pier, opened in 1890. Cecil Newton the LT&SR Company Secretary was a leading light in its promotion, but the LT&SR company was not involved otherwise.

---

adoption of steam boats at the Woolwich and Tilbury ferry crossings, could produce a new and profitable route from London to the large towns of Woolwich and Gravesend, abstracting traffic from the established and busy river steamboats. There was more than just local traffic to be had; the Rosherville Gardens at Gravesend were becoming the number one 'leisure park' of the day, visited by thousands of Londoners daily in the summer season; and the heavy summer traffic to Margate and Ramsgate, at this date travelling by river steamboats throughout, could be enticed into a quicker journey by rail from London to a South Essex pier whence 'railway' steamers could run to the Kent resorts.

In fact it was this summer season traffic to Gravesend, Margate and Ramsgate that was to be the primary magnet to railway promotion in South Essex. A second, but rather subsidiary, target was Southend; some of the 1840s schemes did not bother with a continuation to Southend. A third, and more speculative, prospect was the possibility of establishing a new railway-connected dock which would enable seagoing ships to avoid the congested, time-consuming and all too often fog-shrouded journey up to the London docks.

THE CONTENDERS
Railway development to the east of London began in the 'Little Mania' of 1836, with the authorisation of three schemes quite separate in origin and with quite different aims - the Eastern Counties Railway, the Commercial Railway (renamed London & Blackwall Railway in 1839) and the Thames Haven Dock & Railway (Map 1).

The **Eastern Counties** with a line authorised from London (Shoreditch) to Yarmouth via Chelmsford, Colchester, Ipswich and Norwich, was planned from the start to be the greatest line in East Anglia. Following as it did one of the country's busiest coach roads, it seemed as certain of success as any railway in East Anglia could be. In the event, however, it was to be plagued with financial and constructional problems; and after opening to Romford in 1839, Brentwood in 1840 and Colchester in 1843, it gave up any attempt to proceed beyond. It was only in the late 1840s that it became clear that the ECR was after all to become East Anglia's leading railway.

The **London & Blackwall** line was to be a mere three miles in length, from the edge of the City at Minories to Blackwall Pier on the Thames. Many of the river steamers from London Bridge to Woolwich, Gravesend and Margate already called at Blackwall en route, for the benefit of East London passengers. The London & Blackwall Railway scheme was conceived in the hope that, because the railway journey to Blackwall would be much quicker than the circuitous six-mile river journey around the Isle of Dogs, most of the steamer companies would make Blackwall their terminus once the railway opened, with all the London passengers travelling to Blackwall by train.

The L&BR line opened in 1840, worked by a curious rope-haulage system (and in 1841 was extended a quarter of a mile from Minories to Fenchurch Street in the heart of the City). It gained a tolerable traffic, but most of the steamer companies actually carried on running from London Bridge, as it was found that it was generally only the steamer passengers for the nearer destinations who considered the time-saving obtained by using the L&BR worthwhile.

The **Thames Haven Dock & Railway Co** proposed a dock and pier at Shellhaven on the Corringham marshes, this

being the lowest point on the north bank of the Thames where there was deep water close inshore. It was hoped to attract largescale coal importing at the dock and steamer services to Margate and Ramsgate at the pier. The THD&R Co had originally proposed a railway line of their own all the way from a London terminus to Thames Haven, but when the ECR proposals assumed a definite form the THD&R Co had been persuaded to start their line from the ECR at Romford instead.

Dependent as it was on the success of the proposed new dock, the THD&R Co scheme was much the most 'speculative' of these 1836 proposals, and, at a time when many other very solid-looking railways were being authorised elsewhere in the country, it never managed in the 1830s and 1840s to raise enough capital to enable more than a small and useless start on its works.

The ECR and L&BR were built at 5ft gauge (and the THD&R Co would have had to follow suit), but were converted to standard gauge in 1844 and 1849 respectively. At the same time in 1849 the L&BR also substituted locomotives for rope haulage.

These three companies authorised in 1836 were to become the contenders in the 1840s in an off-and-on battle to 'claim' Thames-side Essex, which eventually ended in the Act for the 'London, Tilbury & Southend' line - in which all three had some part - in 1852. In this contest, the three players had, again, very different motives. The ECR was primarily out to consolidate its position as the leading East Anglian company by keeping others out of the vacant spaces left on the map. The L&BR wanted to make new connections to bring further traffic to its line, its situation being rendered all the more pressing by the authorisation in 1844/5 of the ECR (as it soon became) line from Stratford to North Woolwich, and in 1845 of the South Eastern's North Kent line to Gravesend; when opened in 1847 and 1849 respectively these two lines took away much of the L&BR's (and the steamboats') existing traffic by giving Woolwich and Gravesend direct railway links for the first time. The THD&R Co simply wanted to find some way of getting its moribund scheme off the ground.

The years after 1836 were generally unpropitious for railway promotion, so it was not until 1842 that the first additional scheme for South Essex was developed. This came from the THD&R Co who had not enjoyed good relationships with the ECR for most of the period since 1836, and accordingly decided in 1842 to revert to their original scheme of an independent line from London, now starting from the L&BR at Stepney and passing through Plaistow, Barking, Dagenham, and South Ockendon. They threw in a branch from Ockendon to Tilbury - an idea which they had previously toyed with in late 1836, and were to push again later - hoping no doubt to attract thereby the support of the L&BR. This scheme was deposited for the 1843 and 1844 parliamentary sessions, but in the event the impoverished THD&R Co did not proceed with the Bills in either year. In 1844 the ECR considered a Tilbury line, but did not proceed with it.

In 1845, the L&BR secured an Act for a line from Stepney to the ECR at Bow Junction. This had been promoted as part of an L&BR line to Epping but ECR opposition had seen off the Bow to Epping section in parliament, on a promise that the ECR would themselves build an Epping branch and book the passengers to Fenchurch Street via Bow Junction (which eventually happened, but not until 1856). The Stepney-Bow section was proceeded with by the L&BR and opened in 1849, only to find that the ECR refused to put in the junction at Bow (for which see later). From 1854 this Stepney-Bow line was to be used by 'LT&S' trains.

THE SESSION OF 1846
The 'mania' years saw schemes for South Essex as prolific as those elsewhere in the country. 1846 was - if one discounts an abortive 'Southend and Hole-Haven Railway' of 1835/6 which had been squeezed out by the THD&R Co - the first year in which railways were promoted to Southend, and also (given the stillborn nature of the 1842-4 THD&R Co schemes) the first time that the idea of building a railway to Tilbury was seriously debated in public. There were four competing schemes.

The **London & South Essex Railway** was for all practical purposes promoted by the L&BR, although dressed up as a separate company. The L&BR had in fact discussed the possibility of 'a railway to Southend with a branch to Tilbury Fort', as a next stage in their expansion, back in 1844 when the Epping line was being planned. The 'London & South Essex' was to begin at the site of the future Gas Factory Junction on the Stepney-Bow line and run through Barking to a junction south of Upminster, whence one branch continued to a pier at Tilbury, and the other to Southend via Wickford and Rochford (with a third branch off it to a Wallasea Ness pier on the Crouch). The plans were prepared by Joseph Locke, who was by this date acting generally as the L&BR's engineer, and the estimate was £800,000. A deal was arranged with the THD&R Co under which the latter would sell out to the L&BR.

The **London & Southend Railway** was an independent initiative and proposed a line from Shenfield to Billericay, Wickford, Rayleigh, Rochford, and Southend - the first proposal for a line on this axis. This was a sensible scheme but got squeezed out by circumstances, the promoters being told by the ECR Board in January 1846 that they could not support the scheme 'this year'.

The **Eastern Counties Junction & Southend Railway** was another independent scheme looking for ECR support. From a junction with the ECR at Romford it would have run (more or less following the THD&R Co's 1836 Act line, which was no doubt seen as pretty well moribund by this date) to a point near South Ockendon where it, like the L&BR's scheme, split into Tilbury and Southend/Wallasea branches. Unfortunately, the promoters deposited their parliamentary plans a day too late and so were doomed to failure so far as 1846 was concerned.

Perhaps the most interesting feature of the ECJ&SR in retrospect was that from Fobbing to Southend it was largely on the line of the future 'LT&S' 1852 Act line.

The **North Gravesend Railway** was historically much the most significant of the four schemes of the 1846 session, as it brought into the South Essex scene the two figures who were to be most active in getting the future LT&SR built - the engineer George Parker Bidder and the contractor Samuel Morton Peto. Bidder was at this time engaged in the construction of his Stratford-North Woolwich line, already arranged to be sold to the ECR, and was also engineer (under Stephenson) to the SER's North Kent line (to which the North Gravesend was in many ways a rival project!). He was thus very familiar with the Thames steamer traffic.

The NGR, like the North Woolwich line, was promoted by Bidder himself with the co-operation of his friends on the ECR Board. Three of the NGR's provisional Directors were ECR Directors, and the NGR prospectus spoke openly of the ECR's support. Bidder was naturally an NGR Director himself, so Stephenson was made the NGR's engineer in law, but in fact it was Bidder who did everything and gave the evidence in parliament as 'de facto engineer'. In January 1846 Bidder secured the ECR's agreement to purchase the NGR from him. Peto appeared as an NGR witness in parliament and stated that he was willing to 'take' the line, i.e. build it for non-cash payment.

The NGR would have left the North Woolwich branch at Barking Road (Canning Town), thence swinging east to Barking - this somewhat odd indirect alignment probably being designed to maximise the use of Bidder's North Woolwich line! From east of Barking to its terminus at a Tilbury pier, the NGR ran on the line of the future LT&SR. The estimate was £250,000. Bidder

had no interest in continuing to Southend at this date.

The dropping out of the London & Southend and the Eastern Counties Junction & Southend resulted in the 1846 parliamentary contest being between the London & South Essex and the North Gravesend only. They were considered at length by the same House of Commons committee in May 1846, but on 26th May the committee resolved to throw out both schemes.

Everything was therefore back in the melting pot again. The L&BR Board reassured shareholders at their August 1846 meeting that they would not give up the territory and that 'every effort will be made to retain for the Blackwall proprietary, the traffic of the left bank of the Thames so legitimately their own'. But in the event, although the 'London & South Essex' plans were redeposited in November 1846, no Bill was put down for the 1847 session. The London & Southend promoters also redeposited, but again failed to secure ECR support and were forced to back off. (The London & Southend, and Eastern Counties Junction & Southend, 'companies' were both formally wound up in 1850).

THE ECR'S ATTEMPT TO PROMOTE THE 'LT&S' (1847-8)
The 'LT&S' as actually built in the 1850s was effectively evolved in the autumn of 1846 by the ECR, who realised, after the competition in the 1846 session (in which they had not actually had any scheme in the ECR's own name), that they needed to act in the 1847 session if they were to win the territory.

However, the name 'London Tilbury & Southend' was not in fact used until 1852. The plans deposited by the ECR in November 1846 instead went under the title of 'Eastern Counties Extension, from Ilford to Tilbury Fort and Southend, with a branch from Vange to Battlesbridge'. They were drawn up (not surprisingly) by Bidder. This was the first time that anyone had proposed starting from the ECR at 'Ilford' (i.e. Forest Gate Junction - it was actually on the boundary of West Ham and East Ham parishes and not in Ilford at all, but for some reason the name 'Ilford' was always used prior to 1854). This was a good deal more sensible than the North Gravesend's commencing at Canning Town! It was also the first time - and in this lay its claim to be the true origin of the 'LT&S' as built - that any scheme had sought to serve both Tilbury and Southend by the same line instead of by two separate branches. This meant a somewhat roundabout route to Southend, but a lesser route mileage to be built in total; and Southend was regarded as a less important target than Tilbury. There was also a deliberate aim to keep the line as far away as possible from the existing ECR main line, to maximise the 'new' territory served. The purpose of the Vange-Battlesbridge branch is not clear, unless it were merely to rebut any rival schemes in that area.

Give or take a few yards, this ECR scheme was exactly the 'LT&S' line as eventually authorised in 1852, save that from Forest Gate Junction to Ripple Lane it was on a quite different line to the south of the town of Barking (this was opposed by Barking interests in parliament in 1847 on the grounds that it severed the town from the river). The railway was to be double track (except that the Battlesbridge branch would be single) and the estimate was £500,000. No definite decisions had been made on station sites. Intermediate sidings could if desired be laid in for farmers at any of the level crossings, worked by the resident crossing keepers.

The L&BR's decision not to promote a Bill in the 1847 session left the ECR's scheme as the sole contender for the territory in that session. They did however find themselves opposed by the THD&R Co, who now had ideas of building a Tilbury branch of their own again; the ECR suspected that the THD&R Co were really only opposing in the hopes of getting a high price for agreeing to abandon their schemes altogether. In the House of Commons the ECR put forward the usual parade of farmers and local gentry. Their main witness was David Waddington, the ECR Vice-Chairman since 1845 (when he had been brought in by George Hudson) and a friend of the Bidder/Peto camp. Amongst the ideas mentioned by Waddington were hopes of developing Purfleet for middle-class 'residential' purposes, and of building 'suburban villages' for the

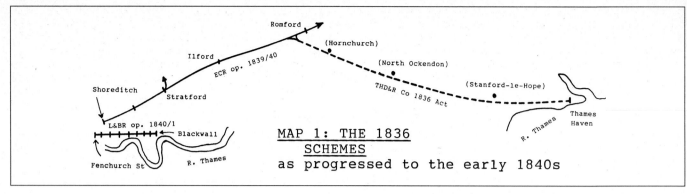

MAP 1: THE 1836
SCHEMES
as progressed to the early 1840s

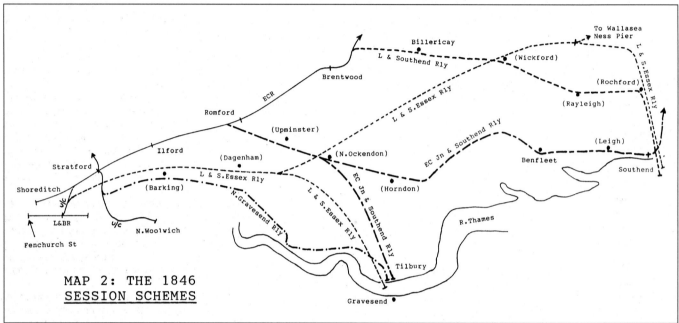

MAP 2: THE 1846
SESSION SCHEMES

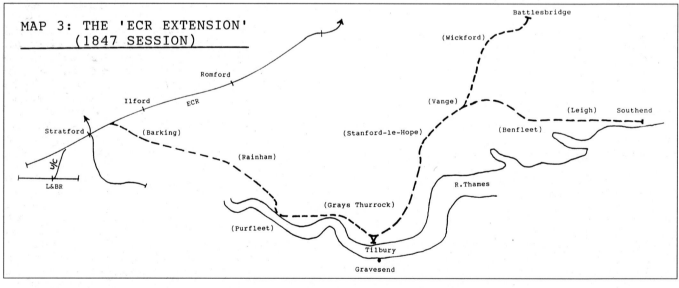

MAP 3: THE 'ECR EXTENSION'
(1847 SESSION)

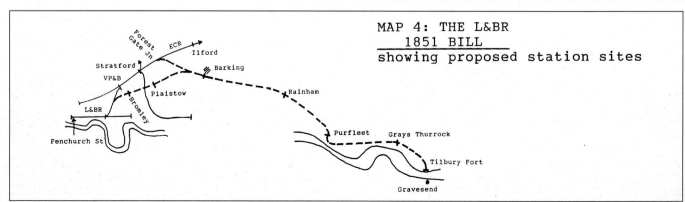

MAP 4: THE L&BR
1851 BILL
showing proposed station sites

All maps approx scale 5 miles to the inch

lower classes up to fifteen miles out of London with special cheap workers' trains for them. Southend could be developed as a resort for 'the poorer classes', although it would 'not have the attractions of Brighton for the higher classes'. Cheap fares would be offered on the line as a whole, thanks to the low construction costs enabled by the easy ground. Even if the 'suburban villages' on the marshes never came off, this is all of interest in showing how the 'LT&S' was conceived of as the 'poor man's railway' right from the start in 1846/7.

The ECR's hopes received a setback when, after a successful passage through the Commons, the Bill became one of a number to be 'suspended' in the 1847 session and carried over to the 1848 session.

In the winter of 1847/8 Bidder managed to secure an agreement with the THD&R Co under which they would abandon the Romford to Mucking section of their 1836 Act line (the powers for which they had kept alive by subsequent extension-of-time Acts) and build only the Mucking to Thames Haven section, with a connection to the ECR line at Mucking. (Although this agreement in itself became void when the ECR's Bill failed, it was to form the basis of the 1852 agreement under which the conflict with the THD&R Co was eventually resolved, as described in Chapter 2).

Unfortunately for the ECR, when their Bill was re-presented in February 1848 it was found that there were irregularities in the subscription lists, as a result of which it failed to pass standing orders in the House of Lords and was perforce abandoned altogether. It will be realised that, but for this unfortunate technicality, the 'LT&S' line would almost certainly have been authorised in 1848 as a purely ECR line and would have had a simple history subsequently as an integral part of the GER. Things were not in the event to be so!

After February 1848 the general post-mania slump, exacerbated in the ECR's case by the chaos in which that company found itself after the ousting of Hudson from the chair in March 1849, put the dampers on any party promoting further schemes in the area for a time, and it was only in 1850 that things started moving again.

THE L&BR'S ATTEMPT TO PROMOTE THE 'LT&S' (1851)
(minus the Tilbury-Southend section)
Although the 1851 scheme was promoted in parliament by the L&BR, it was really Bidder who took the initiative in 1850 to get the idea off the ground again. With the Forest Gate junction still being favoured as the starting point, and with Peto's partner E.L. Betts now Chairman of the ECR, one might wonder why it was the L&BR rather than the ECR that Bidder took the scheme to; however it seems that he may have actually approached the ECR first, as he told the parliamentary committee in 1851 that the ECR had not been able to 'join in' as they were 'in trouble'.

There is no reason to think that Bidder's interest went beyond a desire to see to completion an idea which he had now been pushing since the North Gravesend scheme in 1846, and thereby secure an income for himself as Engineer from a scheme for which the initial plans were effectively already done, and the building of which he could easily look after given that he would be spending much time in the area on his Victoria Dock project anyway. (Although geographically adjacent, the 'LT&S' was not at all related to the Victoria Dock in potential traffic terms).

Bidder now brought Peto (who had already been involved since 1846 as a potential contractor) fully into the promotion of the project, together with the other leading contractor of the day, Thomas Brassey. Peto and Brassey had not worked together before, but during the course of 1850 Bidder brought them into consortium for three of his projects; the Victoria Dock, the Norwegian Grand Trunk Railway, and the Tilbury scheme. 1850, in fact, really represents the date at which contractors at large were forced to start becoming much more actively involved in the promotion of railway schemes, for the simple reason that the vast number of railway works initiated in the 'mania' of 1845/6 were now coming to an end, and the contractors were accordingly being left with idle equipment, without much sign that the public at large were going to promote enough new

schemes to keep them occupied in the 1850s. Peto's large contracts on the ECR had all come to an end in 1848/9, and Brassey's order book had fallen from 10 new contracts for 341 miles of railway in 1845 to a mere one new contract for 13 miles of railway in 1849. As with Bidder there is no reason to think that Peto and Brassey had any particular 'political' interest in building a line to Tilbury as such (although they were subsequently to become involved in plenty of political machinations as a result of it!).

It was no surprise that the L&BR were still keen in 1850/1 on promoting a line into South Essex. Thanks to the ECR's refusal to put in the junction at Bow when the L&BR's Stepney-Bow line opened in 1849, their hopes of getting new traffics had so far been frustrated; and their Gravesend traffic had indeed dropped off, as they had foreseen, since the North Kent line had opened. The number of Gravesend passengers on the L&B line had fallen from 1,046,000 in 1846 to only 526,000 in 1849. (The L&BR's only other hope in 1850 lay in the pending opening of the East & West India Dock & Birmingham Junction Railway, which would bring a passenger traffic from North London into Fenchurch Street).

Bidder had not actually had any connections with the L&BR since 1840/1 (indeed in 1846 he had of course been actively opposing the L&BR in parliament over the rival schemes of that year - but things moved very fast in the railway world in the 1840s, and we should not suppose that they were bearing him grudges over that). It was therefore quite out of the blue that the L&BR Board heard on 9th July 1850 that their Chairman had just had an interview with Bidder

'respecting a proposition for laying down an additional line of rails between the Bow junction and the Stratford junction of the ECR, and for making a line of railway from Ilford to Tilbury Fort, upon the cost of which 6% would be guaranteed by responsible parties in addition to half the profits, and such parties would also guarantee this company against loss on their present Gravesend traffic'.

Seven days later it was confided to them that the 'responsible parties' who were prepared to so 'lease' the line (for details of the proposed lease, see later) were in fact Peto and Brassey.

The L&BR were naturally concerned to know the ECR's views, not least given that they had been in conflict with the ECR for the past year and a half over the Bow junction, and that the Tilbury scheme was wholly dependent not only on that junction now being installed but also on L&BR trains running over ECR metals between there and the Forest Gate junction. However Bidder was able to assure them on 30th July that he 'had a satisfactory meeting with the ECR Directors yesterday', and within the next week he had secured the definite agreement of the ECR to the 'third line' to Stratford (which we may assume was being proposed to meet ECR objections to congestion over this section) and to the use of the ECR line between Bow junction and the Forest Gate junction by L&BR trains for '50% of the receipts proportionate to the mileage'. In securing all this agreement, Bidder was of course helped by the position of E.L. Betts as ECR Chairman. As Peto's partner, Betts was himself to be a co-lessee of the proposed Tilbury line with Peto and Brassey! But even on the ECR, the Chairman could not be seen to be too blatantly furthering his personal interests against the company's interests, so there must have been a persuasion within the ECR Board as a whole that it would be better to have a line, which they seem to have thought themselves unable to promote at this date, built by the L&BR and bringing mileage payments to the ECR, rather than not have it built at all.

It will be noted that (as in 1846) Bidder and Peto were only interested in a line to Tilbury, and were omitting the Tilbury-Southend section from the scheme.

On 8th October 1850, urged on by Bidder, the L&BR Board resolved to proceed with the scheme in the 1851 session, provided that the arrangements with the ECR were secure. Unfortunately, only four weeks later, on 5th November, Betts was forced to resign from the ECR Board - the public reason given was his 'late serious accident' but one suspects that his colleagues' suspicions of duplicity over the Tilbury scheme were not uninvolved! From this date (until March 1851) the ECR were wholly hostile to the Tilbury scheme, as the L&BR soon discovered when a deputation to the ECR Board on 12th November got the reaction that the proposals were 'dangerous to the public and detrimental to the company's interests'.

However Bidder had received 'intimations' of all this, and had reacted by drawing up plans for an additional route from Gas Factory Junction (a location which had just come into being in September 1850, with the opening of the East & West India Dock & Birmingham Junction Railway's line) to Barking, which would render the L&BR's Tilbury scheme quite independent of the ECR. The L&BR Board approved this on 12th November. The Forest Gate Junction line was left in, no doubt in the view that the volatile situation might render it wanted again; and the parliamentary plans deposited at the end of November, under the L&BR's own name, were therefore as shown in Map 4. The Forest Gate Junction - Tilbury section was on the same alignment as the 1847 ECR scheme (including running south of Barking). The 'third line' from Bow Junction to Stratford was omitted. The estimate was £280,000. In true Bidderian economy, the whole line was to be built single track, with the Electric Telegraph being used to regulate trains, and all the stations (Bromley, Plaistow, Barking, Rainham, Purfleet, Grays Thurrock, and Tilbury Fort) being passing places. Bidder claimed that a half-hourly service could be run on this basis and was so confident of this that he proposed to build the earthworks and bridges at single-track width also, as it was not expected that the line would ever have to be doubled! The scheme was referred to colloquially as the 'North Gravesend'.

The arrangements between the L&BR and Peto & Brassey were formalised in an Agreement dated 18th November 1850 under which:-
- Peto & Brassey were to 'indemnify the L&BR against all parliamentary expenses' and pay the cost of Bidder's surveys. (Peto & Brassey originally wanted their parliamentary expenses obligation to be limited to £1,500, but in the event they had to pay £6,000 or more).
- Peto & Brassey were to build the line for the sum estimated by Bidder, and bear any extra costs themselves if this sum proved insufficient.
- Peto & Brassey were to be given a lease of the line on completion for 25 years at a rental of 6% (i.e. pay the shareholders a guaranteed dividend of 6% every year), any profits made above this level being shared 50/50 between Peto & Brassey and the shareholders.
- Peto & Brassey were to decide the timetables and charges for passengers and goods.

Although this 1850 Agreement was in itself rendered void by the failure of the L&BR Bill, it was to be the basis of the 1852 LT&S Agreement under which the LT&S line was actually worked from 1854 to 1875. (It seems that Peto never actually signed the 1850 Agreement - this seems to have been a habit of his as the same thing was to happen with the 1852 Agreement!).

Although small impoverished railway companies often entered into leasing arrangements, it was somewhat unusual for an established company in tolerable financial circumstances to do so. It must have arisen through Bidder and Peto sensing that the L&BR needed reassuring that they would not make a loss on the scheme. From the lessees' viewpoint, such arrangements were, if the more cynical observers of the time are to be believed, usually arranged with the idea that the construction estimate would be on the high side so that the lessees could secure a 'surplus profit' on the construction, the investing of which would more than cover any possible subsequent losses in the working. (Peto Brassey & Betts never did in the event make any annual profits from the LT&SR lease, but this 1850 Agreement would almost certainly have been more profitable to them than that of 1852, because there would have been no 'tolls' to pay for the use of the ECR line).

A special L&BR shareholders' meeting on 3rd December 1850 approved the Bill and the lease, and the Board resolved to take steps to raise the capital. Peto & Brassey intimated that they would take £100,000 in shares themselves.

The next step was the buying off of the likely opposition to the Bill. On 21st January 1851 Tyerman the L&BR Solicitor was able to tell the Board that he had secured an agreement with the Thames Haven Dock & Railway Co, who had given notice of a Bill to revive the powers for their 1836 Act line and add a branch to Tilbury (the latter no doubt primarily as a negotiating move to help their talks with the L&BR). It was now agreed that
- The THD&R Co would abandon their Tilbury branch
- The THD&R Co would abandon the Romford to Mucking section of their 1836 Act line, and build only the Mucking to Thames Haven section
- An Act would be applied for in a future session for a line from Tilbury to Mucking to link the L&BR line with the residual THD&R Co line.

This, mutatis mutandis, was the same as what the THD&R Co had agreed with the ECR in 1847/8. (In the event, the failure of the L&BR's Bill meant that the agreement was once again not proceeded with, and the THD&R Co's 1851 Act actually authorised the renewal of the powers for the whole line from Romford to Thames Haven).

Then on 11th February 1851 a meeting was held with the Gravesend Corporation, the owners of the Gravesend-Tilbury ferry which was a vital part of the L&BR scheme. The Corporation stated that they wished to maintain the management of the ferry, and put various proposals. A committee of L&BR Directors was appointed to discuss further details with the Corporation.

The ECR naturally petitioned against the Bill initially, and much opposition would have been expected from them. However on 20th March 1851 the whole situation was upturned again when Waddington (who had left the ECR Board after Hudson's downfall) was returned to it as Chairman. Waddington was very much an ally of Peto and Bidder and a couple of weeks after his return the ECR's opposition to the Bill was withdrawn, and an agreement come to that the ECR would be given running powers over the new line from Forest Gate Junction to Tilbury and be entitled to promote a Tilbury-Southend extension themselves in a future session.

Despite this favourable turn, all was not going well with the Bill. On 18th March the L&BR Board heard from their Chairman that he had had a meeting with the Railway Commissioners and they had objected to the clauses regarding the Peto & Brassey lease. He feared the Bill would have to be abandoned. Nevertheless it did in fact pass the House of Commons committee. Here the main evidence was given by Arthur Wightman, the L&BR Superintendent, and John Fowler who had been appointed by Bidder as his assistant on the Tilbury scheme, again with plenty of local traders and gentry to back up the case. Wightman gave some interesting figures on the Thames steamer traffic as it stood in 1850 (passengers per annum to and from London)

Purfleet Pier		14,000
Grays Pier		25,000
Rosherville Pier		187,400
Gravesend Town Pier		362,942
Gravesend Terrace Pier		569,366
Southend Pier		25,000
Sheerness	approx	10,000
Herne Bay		15,388
Margate		78,118
Ramsgate	approx	55,000

The L&BR were assuming that the Tilbury line would capture all the Purfleet and Grays traffic, and half the rest of the steamer traffic, plus half the North Kent Railway traffic, which together would give them an annual revenue of £48,070. In addition there would be local traffic from the Essex villages.

On 30th May 1851 Fowler assured the House of Lords committee that there was 'a good understanding' between the ECR and the L&BR over the scheme. But the procedural problems over the lease clauses came to the surface again, and on 2nd June the Lords committee threw out the Bill for this reason.

Just as in 1848, therefore, a purely technical matter only prevented the building of the line, this time as a purely L&BR scheme (which would nevertheless have resulted in it becoming a 'GE' line from 1866 when the GER took over the L&BR).

GEORGE PARKER BIDDER - the portrait dates from 1856 - was born in Moretonhampstead in 1806, the son of a small builder. A child prodigy at mathematical calculation, he toured the country giving demonstrations. At 13 he went to Edinburgh University, supported by a group of gentlemen who felt that he ought to have a fuller education; here he was a contemporary of Robert Stephenson, but it seems that he did not know him well at this stage.

In 1824 he began articles under various surveyors and by the late '20s was working with Rastrick and James Walker, on railway schemes in the north. In 1831-4 he was much involved with the granite tramway along Commercial Road and the Brunswick Wharf at Blackwall, so bringing considerable connections with East London and Thames shipping, at this first stage of his career. In 1835 he married Georgina Harby of Poplar.

In 1834 he went on the staff of the London & Birmingham Railway under Robert Stephenson, with whom he now formed a very close relationship, so much so that in 1835 he went into partnership with Stephenson (lasting until Stephenson's death in 1859). From this time until 1847 Bidder spent most of his time on parliamentary work for Stephenson's railways, rather than design work; his formidable intellect soon led to him being regarded as one of the greatest engineers of his day.

From 1836 to 1840 Bidder and Stephenson were the engineers to the London & Blackwall Railway and it was Bidder who devised the rope-traction system; but once this line was completed they had no further connection with it (until Bidder's approaching them over the Tilbury line in 1850).

Bidder's contacts with the ECR began in 1839 when he became involved with the engineering of the Northern & Eastern Railway to which Stephenson was Engineer, and he had a central role in the negotiations for the takeover of the N&ER by the ECR. In 1842-4 he was more heavily involved in the construction of the Yarmouth & Norwich (to which Stephenson was again Engineer, but did very little in practice). Peto, who Bidder had met on the London engineers' scene around 1828 but without any real contact, was the contractor for both the N&ER and the Yarmouth & Norwich; it was during the work on the latter that Peto and Bidder really got to know each other, and from 1844 on they were always extremely close. Bidder was involved to some extent with most of the ECR's new lines of 1843-9, to most of which Peto was the contractor.

A leading advocate of the Electric Telegraph in its nascent period, Bidder adopted it on the Blackwall to regulate the rope working, and then on the Yarmouth & Norwich to enable efficient single line working, thereby saving money on a line which had originally been planned as double and enhancing his reputation for economy in railway construction. He became a close friend of William Fothergill Cooke the patentee of the telegraph, and it was he who introduced Cooke to Lewis Ricardo who purchased the patents and set up the Electric Telegraph Co in 1846, Bidder being a Director of that company from 1846 right through to nationalisation in 1869.

Around 1842 Mr Blyth the Manager of the West India Dock Co pointed out to Bidder that the Plaistow marshes would make a splendid site for a new dock. Bidder saw this and as a result he made his first foray into railway promotion himself, as the leading figure in the Eastern Counties & Thames Junction Railway (Act 1844) and the North Woolwich Railway (Act 1845) which together built the Stratford-North Woolwich branch, opened fully in 1847 and sold to the ECR. From its passing through empty marshland, this line was initially mocked as 'Bidder's folly'. But Bidder and his associates (including Peto) bought up all the land privately, and by 1849 the dock plans had been finalised

(see below).

In 1847-50 Bidder was Engineer to the North Staffordshire Railway during the construction of its initial system (the NSR and the LT&SR were in fact the only two British railways to which Bidder was de jure Engineer). One of the main contractors on the NSR was Thomas Brassey with whom Bidder had had little involvement up to this date, their only previous contact having been on the Trent Valley line from 1845. He must have now got to know Brassey better, although it seems that he never formed the same close personal relationship with him as he had with Peto.

After the collapse of railway promotion in the UK in 1847, Bidder started taking an interest in promoting overseas projects. This led to him spending much time in the 1850s on the Norwegian and Danish railways (both Bidder/Peto projects), the Danish Gas Company and the Netherlands Lands Enclosure Company.

The Act for the Victoria Dock at North Woolwich, which became regarded as Bidder's greatest work, was obtained in 1850. Peto and his partner E. L. Betts were major subscribers and both became directors of the dock company. The construction contract was let to Peto Brassey & Betts and the dock opened in November 1855. An Act of 1853 had authorised the leasing of the dock to Peto Brassey & Betts from opening. In the event the lease lasted only until 1864 when the Victoria Dock Co sold out to the London & St Katharine Dock Co.

In 1856 Bidder became involved with the Norfolk Railway (of which Peto had been Chairman until 1855), and in 1858 he was elected Chairman, holding that post until the GER amalgamation in 1862 when he was rewarded with a seat on the GER Board. He was very active in GER affairs from 1862 to 1866 when he had to resign, although he was involved again (as a leading GER shareholder) in the company's financial crisis in 1867.

Bidder's involvement in the promotion of the 'LT&S' is discussed in full elsewhere in Chapters 1 and 2. But from 1844 to the 1860s he was a leading figure in East Anglian railway politics at large.

He retired in 1877 to Dartmouth, where he had bought a house in 1860, and died there on 28th September 1878. He is buried at Stoke Fleming nearby. Unlike many child prodigies, he had been able to use his mathematical abilities in a rewarding and successful career.

SAMUEL MORTON PETO, latterly Sir Morton Peto, was born in 1809 and apprenticed to his uncle Henry Peto, a builder. In 1830 Henry Peto died and Peto took over the firm in partnership with his cousin Thomas Grissell. 'Grissell & Peto' erected many public buildings in the 1830s and '40s, including Nelson's column and the new Houses of Parliament. They also became increasingly involved with railway work, starting with the Hanwell-Langley section of the GWR. However Grissell became uneasy about the financial aspects of railway work, and in 1846 the partnership was dissolved, Grissell taking over the building side and Peto the railway work.

Later in 1846 Peto entered into another partnership, with E. L. Betts, which lasted until their bankruptcy in 1866. Other, temporary, consortia were entered into from time to time with others for particular projects.

By the mid-'40s Peto was probably the country's leading railway contractor. In the period 1842-9 he had a particularly large number of contracts with the ECR and the Norfolk

Railway, including almost the whole line from Stratford to Norwich via Ely, Ely-March-Peterborough and St Ives-March-Wisbech, Wymondham-Fakenham, and the Yarmouth & Norwich. This naturally led him to develop other interests in East Anglia of a personal and political nature, so much so that in the 1850s there was hardly an ECR Board meeting that did not have Peto either present in person or by letter, under one or more of his innumerable 'hats'. Often he was in violent conflict with the ECR under one hat, whilst seeking to conspire with them at the same time under another hat. The most significant of his roles were with the LT&S, as Chairman of the Norfolk Railway (until 1855) and in connection with his Lowestoft interests. The last began in 1843 and led to him setting up the Lowestoft Railway & Harbour Co in 1845, which built the Reedham-Lowestoft railway (to which he himself was contractor) opened in 1847. He became Lord of the Manor of Lowestoft and bought Somerleyton Hall as his main residence, rebuilding it in grander style.

In 1847 Peto became MP for Norwich

(Liberal), until 1854 when he was obliged to resign when he took a Government contract for a military railway from Sebastopol to Balaclava, a scheme which he had proposed to the Government himself. It was executed on a no-profit basis and resulted in his being given a Baronetcy. He returned to the House later as MP for Finsbury from 1859 and Bristol from 1865 until forced to resign on his bankruptcy in 1868.

The practice of taking payment in shares rather than cash led to Peto becoming a Director of many railway companies beyond those (notably the East Suffolk) which he had promoted himself. He was for example Chairman of the Chester & Holyhead, Wells & Fakenham, and Severn Valley. These companies had however mostly been taken over by others by the 1860s.

The formation of the GER more or less put an end to Peto's machinations in East Anglia, and in 1861-66 he was primarily involved with the promotion of the London Chatham &

Dover system, for which Peto & Betts, with Crampton, got all the contracts on a non-competitive basis. The whole LC&DR saga became notorious as one of the most blatant examples of a 'contractors' line', and involved massive amounts of 'funny money' which led to Peto & Betts failing with huge debts on the very day of the Overend Gurney Bank collapse, 11th May 1866. However Peto & Betts were allowed to continue to manage their affairs on behalf of the liquidator. Peto was not made personally bankrupt until 1868 when proceedings were brought against him by the LC&DR. He then retired from public life, although he did undertake one or two further railway contracts in the 1870s. He died on 13th November 1889.

Peto was a man of entrepreneurial spirit in both its good and bad aspects; one of those who changed the world, but in the forefront of the (to us) dubious financial dealings that marked railway promotion in the 1850s and 1860s. He received much sycophantic praise as a result of his practice of donating large

sums from his huge personal wealth to charitable causes. But he had few enemies and he enjoyed the friendship and admiration of many of the greatest men of the day.

Peto's partner **Edward Ladd Betts** was born in 1815, the son of William Betts, in Dover. He was apprenticed to a Lincoln builder, and established himself as a contractor by 1835, undertaking much railway work. In 1843 he married Peto's sister Anne.

In 1849-50 Betts was Chairman of the ECR (which many would have regarded as much the same thing as Peto holding the post himself!). But he always took a back seat in dealings with the ECR at other times, hardly ever becoming involved in LT&S matters, which he left to Peto. Indeed he was a much less flamboyant figure than Peto altogether. He lost most of his fortune as a result of the bankruptcy and died in Egypt in 1872 after travelling there in the hope of restoring his ailing health. He is buried at Aylesford near his former residence Preston Hall.

THOMAS BRASSEY was born in Buerton, Cheshire in 1806 and apprenticed to a Chester surveyor. In 1835 George Stephenson gave Brassey the contract for 10 miles of the Grand Junction Railway. Stephenson was soon replaced by Locke as the GJR's Engineer and this was the start of a long association between Brassey and Locke. Brassey was given the contracts for most of Locke's lines, notably the LSWR. In 1841 Brassey gained the contract (again under Locke) for the Paris & Rouen Railway and this was followed by a very large amount of overseas work, Brassey being the first British contractor to venture into overseas railway work to any extent. In East Anglia Brassey (under Locke) built most of the Eastern Union lines in the 1840s.

Most of Brassey's contracts were done with a partner, usually Mackenzie or Ogilvie in the 1840s, and Field or Ogilvie later. However after being 'introduced' to working with Peto & Betts by Bidder in 1850, he also did much subsequent work with them, notably the West End of London & Crystal Palace Railway, ECR Stratford-Hackney branch and Royal Danish Railway under Bidder; and the Hereford Ross & Gloucester, Lyons & Avignon, Grand Trunk

(Canada), East Suffolk, Elizabeth-Linz, Jutland, North Schleswig, Queensland and various New South Wales railways under other engineers, all in the 1852-66 period.

By the 1850s Brassey had probably overtaken Peto as the greatest contractor of his time. He built 6415 miles of railway altogether (of which 4475 were overseas).

Brassey was a very different character to Peto, a quieter and more cautious man who avoided ostentation. His work with Peto seems to have been conducted happily enough, but the two do not appear to have become especially close personally. Although he was inevitably obliged to engage in the financial customs of the day, he was cautious enough in his dealings to enable him to survive the financial crisis of 1866 when so many others went under. He never sought to involve himself in public life and politics, but restricted himself to his job of being the country's most successful railway contractor. The rewards of this approach can be judged from the fact that on his death in 1870 he left £3,200,000 in respect of his property in the UK alone.

Brassey did involve himself to some extent in the management of the LT&SR lease in the 1850s and 1860s, but he left most of that role to Peto.

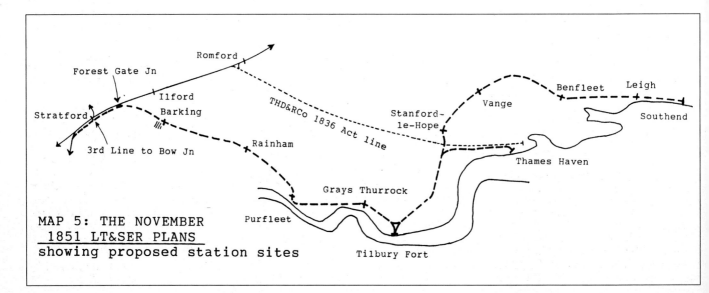

MAP 5: THE NOVEMBER 1851 LT&SER PLANS showing proposed station sites

CHAPTER 2

The London Tilbury & Southend Extension Railway: Promotion, Construction and Opening (1851-6)

THE SUCCESSFUL JOINT PROMOTION OF THE 'LT&S' LINE IN THE 1852 SESSION

When their 1851 Bill was thrown out, the L&BR immediately told the ECR on 3rd June 1851 that they hoped that this loss would not interfere with the 'mutual good feelings' that had now been established, and asked for a meeting to discuss 'future combined efforts'. The ECR were agreeable but as was often the case nothing was done until the autumn when the 30th November deadline for the deposit of parliamentary plans began to loom large.

On 9th September 1851 the L&BR Board asked Bidder to begin negotiations with the ECR on their behalf, and later that month they told the ECR that they proposed to renew their application (i.e. for a line to Tilbury only) in the coming session, and hoped that the ECR would support it. Some of the ECR Directors had, however, now got ideas of an alternative scheme involving separate branches to Southend and Tilbury, and this caused problems when the L&BR and ECR Boards eventually met on 7th October; but the ECR agreed to refer the matter to Bidder for a decision, and he (not surprisingly) recommended in favour of a route to Southend via Tilbury as had been promoted by the ECR in 1847/8. Another meeting between the Boards on 16th October agreed this (the L&BR thereby conceding that the line should continue to Southend instead of stopping at Tilbury). It was also agreed that the line should be jointly promoted by the L&BR and ECR in the 1852 session; that it should be run by a Joint Committee after opening; and that 'the agreement between the (L&B) company and Messrs Peto & Brassey is to form part of the agreement between the two companies'.

On this basis plans were duly drawn up by Bidder and Fowler, and deposited in November 1851 under the name of 'The London Tilbury and Southend Extension Railway' - the first ever use of the 'LT&S' name (the word 'Extension' in the title was to be quietly dropped in 1854). Of course no great amount of survey work was needed, the alignment being exactly as per the ECR scheme of 1847/8 and the L&BR scheme of 1851, save that the Forest Gate Junction to Ripple Lane section was now on a new line running to the north of the town of Barking. The Gas Factory Junction - Barking section was omitted now that the ECR was friendly. A Thames Haven branch was included, no doubt as a negotiating ploy for dealing with the inevitable opposition of the THD&R Co.

It was now intended to build the line double from Forest Gate Junction to Tilbury, and single from Tilbury to Southend (with land and bridges for double, in the usual way). It was also proposed to build a 'third line' for up trains between Forest Gate Junction and Bow Junction (although this was not in fact included in the LT&SER plans, and only came off in part).

The THD&R Co themselves made an approach to the L&BR as soon as they heard of the scheme in October, seeking an agreement on the same lines as had been made in 1847/8 and 1851, i.e. that they should build only the Mucking-Thames Haven section of their line and join the LT&SER at Mucking.

Following this approach the "LT&SER" Thames Haven branch was dropped before the Bill was presented. However the THD&R were actually to oppose in committee all the same (see later).

The Joint Bill was approved by a special L&BR shareholders' meeting on 24th November 1851, and similarly by the ECR shareholders on 4th December.

The legal situation of the joint ownership, as sorted out in October 1851 and incorporated without change in the 1852 LT&SER Act, was somewhat complex. The LT&SER line was to be joint property of the L&BR and ECR companies, but they as companies were not directly the owners of the capital in the normal way of a 'joint line'. The share capital (£400,000 in £10 shares) was instead to be offered to individual existing L&BR and ECR shareholders or, if they did not take it all, to the public at large. Shares Nos 1-20,000 were nevertheless deemed to be part of the capital of the ECR for legal purposes and shares 20,001-40,000 part of the capital of the L&BR. The holders of LT&SER shares were entitled to attend and vote at ECR or L&BR meetings 'upon questions relating to the undertaking' but not on other matters (unless of course they were also normal shareholders in those companies anyway). Correspondingly, ECR and L&BR shareholders who were not also owners of LT&SER shares were not entitled to vote on 'LT&SER' matters even though they might be discussed at the ordinary ECR and L&BR shareholders' meetings! [This rather impractical situation was disposed of by the LT&SR (Amendment) Act 1856 which provided that separate meetings should always be held for LT&SER shareholders thenceforth, the first ordinary half-yearly LT&S shareholders' meeting accordingly taking place in February 1857].

The line was to be run by a Joint Committee of eight members, of whom four were to be appointed by the ECR Board and four by the L&BR Board. The unfortunate LT&SER shareholders were, therefore, not entitled to appoint any Directors at all! - a fact that was to have some impact on the subsequent history of the LT&S, as many shares were in the event taken up by persons who were not existing ECR or L&BR shareholders and so found themselves in a position of powerlessness probably unparalleled elsewhere.

These complexities were too much for Waddington the ECR Chairman who caused confusion at the 4th December ECR shareholders' meeting by stating that the LT&SER was to be 'a separate company' (which it was not until 1862).

The problems that the L&BR had encountered in the 1851 session, from parliament's reluctance to allow Acts for the building of a line to incorporate powers for the lease or sale of it, meant that the two companies were now very reluctant to admit to the proposed Peto Brassey & Betts lease this time around. (Betts' name was always included from this time on; he would always have been involved anyway, but now that he no longer sat on the ECR Board it was presumably considered acceptable for his name to be formally included as well). When the shares were offered in December 1851, the two Boards would not give any definite guarantee that 6% would be paid each year - they could not, because the lease could not, they now realised, safely be formalised until after they had got their Act. But, trying to have their cake and eat it, they stated that 'no alteration had taken place in the intention of the parties' since the previous year! Waddington would not even tell the 4th December ECR meeting who the proposed lessees were, although some of them naturally already knew. A Mr Maclaurin commented 'We have had enough of contractors ... they will take care to have a good price for the works ... the Southend line could be made for one half the proposed capital'. There were several complaints about lack of clear information and it was perhaps no surprise in the circumstances that the ECR Board report of August 1852 stated that 'very few' ECR shareholders had actually taken up LT&SER shares. In the parliamentary committee hearings the witnesses tried to suppress Peto's involvement, and the official line was that the shareholders would be free to choose, after the Act, whether to allow a lease or not.

Peto and Brassey and Betts had in fact put down for £40,000 of shares each; Bidder and Fowler for £10,000 each; and various of the L&BR Directors for £56,000 between them, which together amounted to half the total capital.

On 23rd December 1851 Peto Brassey & Betts threw a spanner in the works by informing Bidder that, whilst they were 'willing to execute the line from Ilford to Tilbury Fort at a price to be fixed by (Bidder)', and to lease the line at 6% after opening, they 'declined at present to go into the question of guarantees upon the portion of the line between Tilbury and Southend'. This highlighted a problem that had no doubt been fudged in October when the agreement between the ECR and L&BR had been thrashed out, viz the previous arrangements with Peto Brassey & Betts, which had been deemed to be part of that agreement, had not been in relation to a line to Southend at all, but only for a line to Tilbury! The immediate response from the ECR to this statement by the lessees was a letter from Maynard the ECR Solicitor, to the effect that the ECR were 'determined to withdraw from the further prosecution of the Bill in consequence'.

Peto Brassey & Betts sought to make out that they were reluctant to get involved in the Tilbury-Southend section because the ECR 'had shown so little disposition to support the proposals for a line in that direction'. But all other evidence suggests that it was in reality the ECR who had always wanted a continuation to Southend, and Bidder and Peto who had preferred a Tilbury-only line. The days after Christmas naturally saw Bidder and the L&BR trying to patch the show together again, and by January the matter was resolved, with Peto Brassey & Betts agreeing to work the whole line.

At the same period, the ECR and L&BR were also discussing constructively for the first time the question of the still-not-installed Bow Junction, which 'LT&S' line trains would have to use to reach Fenchurch Street. Both parties now agreed that it would be desirable also for ECR suburban trains from the North Woolwich and Colchester lines to use Fenchurch Street, which was better-sited for the City than Bishopsgate; and as a result the ECR (which had always insisted previously, when they had not wanted to use it for their own trains, that the junction at Bow would be 'dangerous') now quite cast from their minds the supposed danger! But it was clear that, with ECR and 'LT&S' line trains using Fenchurch Street in addition to the existing Blackwall and North London services, the terminus would need enlarging. An agreement between the ECR and L&BR dated 12th February 1852 provided for this (the ECR to pay 5% interest on the cost of that part of the work needed for their services) and gave the ECR the necessary running powers into Fenchurch Street. The work at Fenchurch Street was then carried out in 1852/3. Whilst this was being done, neither party had any need for the junction at Bow to be installed in the immediate term, so it was left until about January 1854.

The L&BR also had to construct a 'third line' for up trains between Stepney and Fenchurch Street (their 1846 Act had actually empowered four lines over this section); this experienced delays and was not brought into use until 1856.

In parliament, where the usual parade of local witnesses were put forward at the committee hearings in April and May 1852, the LT&SER Bill underwent 'very severe' opposition from the North Kent Railway (whose vested interest in relation to the Gravesend traffic was obvious enough) and, until a last-minute agreement of 3rd June 1852 (discussed later in this chapter),

from the THD&R Co via a landowner. But the ploy of suppressing the lease worked, and, after seven years of frustrated attempts, the London Tilbury and Southend Extension Railway Act 1852 received the Royal Assent on 17th June 1852.

SETTING UP THE JOINT COMMITTEE

The LT&SER Joint Committee met for the first time on 6th July 1852. The two companies had appointed as their representatives on the Committee:-

ECR

David Waddington (the ECR Chairman)
Richard Paterson (the ECR Deputy Chairman)
Lord Alfred Paget
Samuel Anderson

L&BR

James Nugent Daniell (the L&BR Chairman)
William Haigh (the L&BR Deputy Chairman)
Joseph Bishop
Josiah Wilson

Daniell was appointed Chairman of the Joint Committee (and Anderson Deputy Chairman). The L&BR Directors on the Committee were to remain fairly stable over the years to come, but the ECR's members changed frequently in accord with the many revolutions in the ECR Board itself!

The officers to the Committee were

Secretary - John Fisher Kennell (the L&BR Secretary)

Architect & Surveyor - William Tite (Tite, who had manifold interests in railway politics, was Architect & Surveyor to the L&BR, and also to Peto; he is best remembered today for his LSWR work).

Engineer - G. P. Bidder (now formally appointed).

This, with the Chairman and Secretary both L&BR men, gave a distinct 'L&B' bias to the whole set up, a situation that was strengthened in 1853 when Arthur Wightman the L&BR's 'Superintendent and Traffic Manager' was appointed by Peto Brassey & Betts to be also Manager of the LT&S line.

THE PETO BRASSEY & BETTS CONTRACT

At their 27th July 1852 meeting, the Joint Committee resolved to enter into a contract for the building of the line with Peto Brassey & Betts, for £400,000. Peto, who was always to take much the most active role of the three lessees in dealings over the LT&S, was present at this meeting and agreed (subject to matters of detail) to take the contract at this price. However, just as all was about to be finalised, Peto then wrote on 3rd August to say that the contract would only give 4% profit at this price and 'we are not disposed to execute the works for so small a margin'. He wanted a 10% profit and proposed that the contract sum be increased to £425,000, with £25,000 of the £100,000 Debentures (authorised by the 1852 Act in addition to the share capital) being now raised to cover the excess. The Joint Committee expressed 'much surprise' at Peto's new demand, but agreed to it nevertheless.

The Agreement was dated 10th August 1852 and was approved by the ECR and L&BR Boards, the Joint Committee, and a Special Meeting of LT&SER shareholders, all on that day. It was essentially the same as the previous November 1850 L&BR/Peto & Brassey agreement, and provided that Peto Brassey & Betts should construct the line and take a lease of it for 25 years from 1st January 1853 (subsequently changed to 21 years from 3rd July 1854 - see below). They were to pay 6% interest on the share capital, i.e. £24,000 per annum once the full £400,000 was raised, and also the annual interest on the Debentures. If the profit in any year exceeded this, the 'surplus' was to be shared between the lessees and the shareholders (in the event there never was any 'surplus' profit). The costs of obtaining the Act, and the annual running costs of the Joint Committee (not a large sum) were also to be paid by the lessees.

The construction of the line was to be completed in 18 months (this, as usual, was not achieved!) with double track to Tilbury and single beyond. Ten stations were to be built (at the sites shown in Map 5 here), plus a pier with a floating landing stage at Tilbury, and all other necessary structures and fittings.

It should be noted that in August 1852 the two companies did not actually have any statutory power to lease the line (although they were of course perfectly entitled to give a contract for construction). This had to be sought subsequently, and was obtained in the London Tilbury & Southend Railway Deviation and Amendment Act 1854; this Act received the Royal Assent on 3rd July 1854 and for this reason the lease had legally to commence from this date only, although in reality Peto Brassey & Betts leased the line from its first opening in April 1854. It is nowhere stated why it was decided to alter the period of the lease from 25 years to 21.

Reference was made in Chapter 1 to Peto's seeming reluctance to actually sign agreements. In April 1861 the LT&S Joint Committee 'ascertained with much surprise and regret that the lease of this railway has not been executed'. The 1852 Joint Committee minutes state clearly that the two companies had put their seals to the Agreement, so there is no doubt that it was Peto who had not signed; indeed, when the matter was taken up with Peto in 1861, it resulted in his bringing up a list of points on which he still disagreed! The sealing of the Agreement was eventually effected in March 1863.

There were to be two subsequent Agreements with Peto Brassey & Betts when further capital had to be raised; one in June 1856 in relation to extra works on the main line and the purchase of the THD&R Co, and one in July 1856 for the building of the Gas Factory Junction - Barking line. These are both discussed in more detail later.

THE WORKING AGREEMENT WITH THE ECR
Although many 'lessees' of railways ran the trains themselves with their own stock, Peto seems to have disliked this method, and it was known that Peto Brassey & Betts did not intend to acquire stock to run the LT&S train service directly. In November 1852 they asked both the L&BR and the ECR if they would tender for running the trains as agents. The L&BR were not interested, possibly because their existing locomotive establishment was so limited; it is quite clear that the ECR, which had been doing costings for the job three months earlier, was the 'intended' candidate. Everything was sorted out very quickly, Waddington telling the Joint Committee on 21st December 1852 that Peto Brassey & Betts had accepted the ECR's tender, although the formal agreement, for 21 years with a review after 7 years, was (in the way of such things) dated later, 25th March 1854.

The basis of the agreement was that the ECR was to be paid
- 8d per mile for locomotives on passenger trains
- 10d per mile for locomotives on goods trains
- 0.54d per mile for passenger coaches
- 0.35d per mile for brakevans, horseboxes and carriage trucks
- 0.32d per mile for trucks in goods trains
no passenger train to exceed 15 vehicles and no goods train to exceed 35 vehicles. The lessees were to provide 'sheds and sidings' and water for locomotives.

The locomotives and stock for the LT&S line were all built new at Stratford; J.V. Gooch the ECR Locomotive Superintendent told the ECR Board on 30th December 1852 that he wished to get on with this urgently on account of rising prices for materials. By July 1855 the ECR had spent £47,159 building 10 passenger tank locomotives, 2 goods tender locomotives and 61 coaches for the LT&S line.

The prices in the Agreement were very much on the low side and it is clear that the whole arrangement was a cosy one between Waddington and Peto. In 1855 it became the subject of an investigation by ECR shareholders (see Chapter 3).

It will be seen that the whole of the arrangements in relation to the LT&S line were of a peculiar and convoluted kind. It was a railway owned jointly (in an abnormal way at that) by two companies, leased to contractors, but with the train services run by one of the owning companies as agent to the lessees! All this was of course the result of a need to put together something that placated all interests at the various crisis points when they might otherwise have fallen out.

BUILDING THE LINE TO TILBURY
The LT&S was of course a very easy line to build, with no major engineering structures and limited earthworks.

Work seems to have begun about September 1852 and was naturally concentrated initially on the Forest Gate - Tilbury section. On 21st October the ECR Board approved the putting in of the junction at Forest Gate 'and auxiliary signals with a cottage for two men to be at once appointed to the duties', all at Peto Brassey & Betts' expense. An ECR 'General Order' of January 1853 then informed staff that the junction and signals were now in use. Peto Brassey & Betts were also building the ECR's Stratford-Hackney Wick line at this date (the contract had been agreed in October 1852); this line was entirely on embankment and as a result Peto Brassey & Betts wished to bring 'cut' from the LT&S line over the ECR for use as 'fill' on the Hackney line. The ECR Officers' Committee on 26th January 1853 discussed the arrangements for running the 'ballast trains between Tilbury Fort Junction and Stratford', which were to be hauled by ECR locomotives 'on hire' to Peto Brassey & Betts. A 'signalman' was to ride on the last wagon of every such train, 'properly provided with signals'! One wonders how it was that a surplus of earth was actually available from the LT&S line; although the first mile from Forest Gate Junction was in cutting, and there were further short cuttings at Barking, Purfleet, and Grays, the great majority of the line was on low embankment across the marshes which one might have expected to use up such 'cut' as was available.

The works were supervised by Bidder and Fowler. On 20th June 1853 they reported to the Joint Committee that work as far as Tilbury was being 'carried on with great activity' and that they saw 'no reason to doubt that this section of line will be ready by 1st September 1853', a surprising piece of over-optimism from Bidder who was known for meeting his targets (especially given that there are no subsequent reports of any particular cause of delay). On 10th October the Joint Committee were treated to a tour of the works by the contractors, and in December Kennell sent the first notice of opening to Tilbury to the Board of Trade. In mid-January 1854 Peto stated that the line could be opened to Tilbury by 28th February and indeed would be complete to three miles beyond Tilbury (Muckingford) which section however there would be no traffic purpose in opening at this stage. In the event the line opened on 13th April. One of the last jobs to be done was the fixing of the pontoons at Tilbury, and dredging there; given the overwhelming importance of the Gravesend traffic it would probably have been seen as futile to open the line without the ferry service, so this may well have been what delayed the opening.

It will be recalled that it had been intended in 1852 to put in a 'third line' for up trains between Forest Gate Junction and Bow Junction, the idea being that up trains were less likely to be running to time than down trains. This, however, emerged instead as a third line between Stratford and Bow Junction only, for use by down trains, by which means *down* trains from Fenchurch Street would not have to cross the path of up Bishopsgate trains at Bow Junction. The ECR's Woodford & Loughton Branch Act 1853 had in fact made the provision of such a third line compulsory before the Loughton line (whose trains were to run mainly from Fenchurch Street) opened. The ECR's Traffic Committee of 31st May 1853 ordered work on the Stratford-Bow third line to proceed, and in February 1854 it was reported complete. With the Bow Junction itself now laid in at last, and the Fenchurch Street station enlargements now finished, all was ready for the 'LT&S' passenger trains. These, in reflection of the joint ownership, were to run in two portions, from Fenchurch Street and Bishopsgate, joining at Stratford for the run to Tilbury.

The ceremonial opening of the LT&S line to Tilbury took place on Tuesday 11th April 1854 with 'the Directors and a large party of friends proceeding in a special train along its

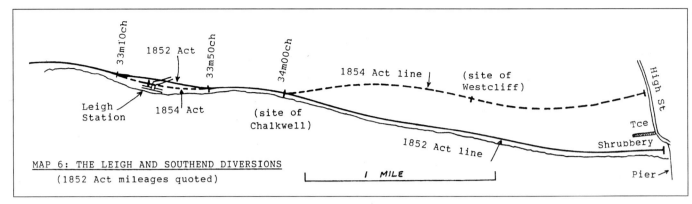

MAP 6: THE LEIGH AND SOUTHEND DIVERSIONS
(1852 Act mileages quoted)

1 MILE

whole length, from the new termini at Fenchurch Street'. The Board of Trade inspection by Captain Wynne was also carried out on this day, and, all being satisfactory, the public opening was on 13th April 1854, the Thursday of the Easter weekend when a good Gravesend traffic was to be expected.

The initial 'LT&S' passenger services are discussed later in this chapter. Goods services (which would appear to have begun on the same date, although this is nowhere specifically stated) are dealt with an Appendix in Vol. 2.

THE LEIGH AND SOUTHEND DIVERSIONS

Work at the eastern end of the line was held up by two important changes of route. The line at Leigh went back to Bidder's autumn 1846 surveys for the 1847/8 ECR scheme, but on 25th October 1853 the Joint Committee were faced with a report from Bidder and Fowler stating that further inspection of the ground had convinced them that the 1852 Act route would involve great difficulties (because it went 'through a steep hillside in a clay cutting', as Bidder said on a subsequent occasion). They had therefore surveyed a diversion, which the Committee approved. This involved running the line very close to the backs of the houses on the north side of the High Street, removing their long gardens. The new route would probably have been objected to as a disaster in amenity terms had the properties in question been occupied by middle-class people, but they were not!

More importantly, it was now sought to delete the last two miles of the 1852 Act route ending in a terminus at the Southend pierhead, and replace this stretch with a wholly new line inland to a terminus on the west side of the High Street. This involved a steep gradient up, but was to prove a fortunate decision in retrospect. It was probably motivated by a feeling that the protection clauses which the occupiers of the superior houses in the Royal Terrace at Southend had obtained in the 1852 Act, would prove impracticably constricting to the operation of the railway. The 1852 Act had provided, inter alia, that

'The said companies shall not obstruct, interfere with, or injure the Bathing in the Sea by means of Machines on the sea beach and shore in front of the Shrubbery'

'The said companies shall not nor will, by means of their said railway and works, and the use thereof, make or cause any Nuisance to the Inhabitants or Occupiers of the Houses on the Terrace at Southend'

'All engines having to blow off their steam for the purpose of ceasing from Work shall be driven or taken to a distance of not less than Half a Mile from the said Terrace Houses, and the ground called the Shrubbery, before such blowing off of their steam shall be commenced'.

It was also forbidden to erect 'any fixed or stationary Engine or Engine House' within half a mile of the Terrace.

The prospect of continual conflict from all this, and perhaps also doubts over the wisdom of building the line directly on the foreshore (it had not been decided whether to do this on piles or embankment), made the inland route desirable.

The Leigh and Southend diversions were authorised by the London Tilbury & Southend Railway Deviation and Amendment Act 1854, to which reference was made previously in the context of the Peto Brassey & Betts lease.

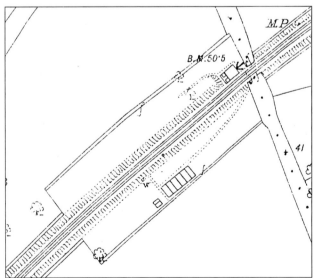

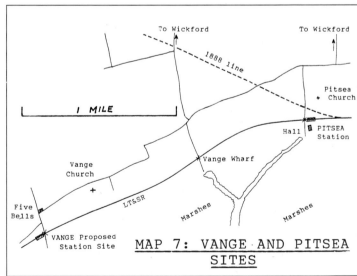

MAP 7: VANGE AND PITSEA SITES

VANGE STATION

The precise site of the 'Vange' station specified in the August 1852 Peto Brassey & Betts contract was almost certainly at what has latterly been known as 'Fobbing Crossing'. This was a reasonably sensible site, being close to the main road, convenient for Fobbing and Langdon Hills, and as near to being halfway between the adjacent stations at Stanford-le-Hope and Benfleet as

any site on a public road. The 1864 survey 25" map reproduced here shows the Vange station site with the land bought and fenced off for the station (and also shows the 1854 keeper's cottage at the level crossing). However the station was never built.

In May 1854 there was a public meeting in Wickford where people were dissatisfied at the prospect of having to go five miles to the nearest station (Vange) when the railway actually passed within 3½ miles of their town. They sent a memo-

rial to the Joint Committee asking for the station to be built instead at Vange Wharf, a mile to the east of the Vange site (and a mile nearer Wickford). The Engineers were asked to report, and it was decided in the event to build the station still further east at Pitsea. There was no 'village' at Pitsea (nor was there at Vange) but it was perhaps the better site given that the Wickford traffic was important to the LT&S (until the GER line opened) in this otherwise sparsely-populated area.

There was also a diversion at Vange, but this was minor enough to be authorised by the magistrates.

BUILDING THE LINE FROM TILBURY TO SOUTHEND

Although much work had been done east of Tilbury by April 1854 (and indeed Peto had reported the Tilbury-Muckingford section nearly complete in January), nothing could be done beyond Hadleigh until after the 1854 Act was passed in July, so it was clear that a 'staged' opening would take place.

Further changes to the scheme were authorised by the Joint Committee on 6th June 1854, when Peto attended to read a report from Fowler recommending
- double line instead of single between Tilbury and Thames Haven Junction (the single line over this section was already laid, although not yet open to public traffic)
- stations between Thames Haven Junction and Southend (sic - he meant Leigh) 'should be constructed as for a double line, and every station or nearly so at once made a passing place'
- double track from the start between Leigh and Southend (plus additional works at stations between London and Tilbury). The Engineers were asked to cost these works, and produced an estimate of £55,000. There was a special shareholders' meeting on 10th November 1854 to approve the raising of the £75,000 residue of the Debentures authorised by the 1852 Act, to pay for these works.

The openings beyond Tilbury - again these are the dates for passenger traffic, with the implication that goods began on the same date - were:-

Tilbury to Stanford-le-Hope (which was the first worthwhile traffic objective beyond Tilbury) on Monday 14th August 1854, after being inspected by Major (as he now was) Wynne on 29th July. There was no ceremony at this, or the later, openings. This section was opened as single - except that Tilbury South Junction to East Junction may have been double from the start - but was doubled to Thames Haven Junction about May 1855.

Tilbury West Junction to Tilbury East Junction - no definite date can be quoted for this. If the 1860s practice of backing London-Southend trains into Tilbury via East Junction, so that they could then depart for Southend without the locomotive having to run round, and vice-versa, was followed from the start, then this curve would have 'opened' on 14.8.1854. It was certainly used by Thames Haven trains from 7.6.1855. It was probably double track from the start.

Thames Haven Junction to Thames Haven on 7th June 1855 - see below for details. This was a single line and remained so.

Stanford-le-Hope to Leigh on Sunday 1st July 1855, including the stations at Pitsea and Benfleet. Wynne had inspected this on 16th June. It was single (from Thames Haven Junction to Leigh) with Pitsea as the only passing place, although there were no timetabled crossings. The exact method by which the various single-line sections were being worked is not clear, but Wynne took a dislike to it, and as a result Peto told the Joint Committee on 5th June 1855 that 'owing to the restrictions imposed by the Board of Trade on the working of single lines of railway, he felt it would be absolutely necessary to double the line from the junction with the Thames Haven Railway to Southend'.

The doubling of the Thames Haven Junction - Leigh section (Leigh to Southend having already been authorised as double track, as noted above) was now approved and effected, and the second line brought into use early in May 1856, so that the whole of the main line was now double.

From the opening to Leigh, all trains were met at Leigh by 'omnibuses' to convey passengers on to Southend.

Leigh to Southend opened on Saturday 1st March 1856, after an inspection by Wynne in late February. It was double from the start.

THE THD&R CO AGREEMENT AND THE BUILDING OF THE THAMES HAVEN BRANCH

As noted above, a formal agreement between the ECR and L&BR, and the Thames Haven Dock & Railway Company, had been made dated 3rd June 1852 on the previously anticipated

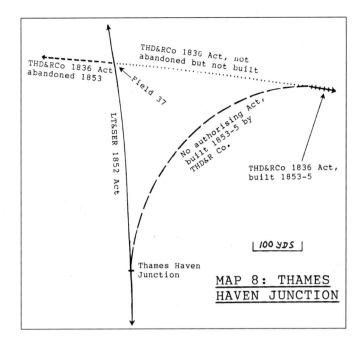

MAP 8: THAMES HAVEN JUNCTION

basis i.e. that the THD&R Co would build only the 'Mucking' to Thames Haven section of their line and abandon the rest. They were also to build wharves at Thames Haven (not the dock, which never did come to be). This agreement was approved by the LT&SER shareholders on 14th September 1852.

The Thames Haven Dock & Railway Act 1853 authorised the abandonment of the 1836 Act line between Romford and Field 37 in the parish of Mucking i.e. the point where it crossed the LT&S line. The THD&R Co's capital was reduced as a result.

The LT&SR Deviation & Amendment Act 1854, already referred to in other contexts, authorised the sale of the remaining section of line and the wharves, when the line had been completed as single track and £10,000 spent on the wharves, to the ECR and L&BR jointly, to form an integral 'part of the undertaking of the London Tilbury & Southend Extension Railway'. The purchase price was £48,000 (which became £49,500 in the event after adding interest). The 1854 Act authorised an additional £52,000 LT&S share capital to cover this.

The Thames Haven branch and the wharves were built by Peto Brassey & Betts under a separate contract between them and the THD&R Co agreed in August 1853. At Mucking a 'curve' had to be built to get from the LT&S at 'Thames Haven Junction' to the THD&R Co's line; although outside the limits of deviation of any past Act, this was built without specific sanction. The terminus of the line at Thames Haven was also at a different point from that authorised in 1836. The THD&R Co's Engineer in charge of the works was George Berkley (who was also the L&BR's Engineer by this date).

By the spring of 1855 the works were nearing completion, and on 7th March the THD&R Co Directors and Berkley visited the site with Arthur Wightman the LT&S Manager 'for the purpose of inspecting the works previous to the transfer of them to the LT&S Company ' (sic). The railway was inspected by Wynne on 27th April, and was opened on 7th June 1855 - nineteen years after the passage of the Act authorising it! The only traffic initially was the daily 'boat trains' from Fenchurch Street for Margate, and even this was, one feels, something of a justification rather than a necessity, since the Margate boats had been picking up London passengers from Fenchurch Street at Tilbury in 1854, and Thames Haven was only marginally closer to Margate. (These Margate trains ran to Thames Haven until 1880). In reality the Thames Haven branch was a white elephant that had only come into being as a result of politics, to buy off the THD&R Co's opposition.

The sale of the line was approved by the THD&R Co shareholders on 2nd July 1855, and by the LT&S shareholders the next day.

The deed of sale was dated 8th September 1855 (so for the first three months the line, although worked by 'LT&S' trains, still belonged legally to the THD&R Co).

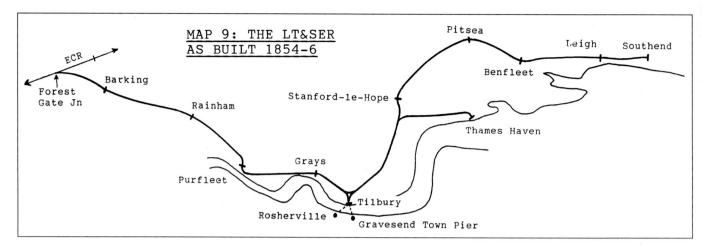

MAP 9: THE LT&SER
AS BUILT 1854-6

The THD&R Co still existed as a company. There was a stormy discussion at their August 1855 shareholders' meeting as to whether they should sell all their remaining land, or continue with the project of building a dock. The latter view prevailed, and the Thames Haven Dock Company's Act 1856 authorised the construction of a dock to the west of the station, on a lesser scale than the 1836 dock proposals, plus a change in the company's name. However they still found it impossible to raise any money, and by another Act in 1861 the dock project was abandoned and the company's unhappy 25 year old history terminated. There must have been many who were surprised to see its having resulted in even a partial success!

On 30th June 1856 a further agreement (mentioned briefly earlier) was made between the ECR & L&BR and Peto Brassey & Betts, under which the £52,000 additional share capital authorised by the 1854 Act for the purchase of the Thames Haven line and wharves, plus a further £60,000 share capital authorised by the London Tilbury & Southend Railway (Amendment) Act 1856 for other works, were brought within the terms of the 1852 Peto Brassey & Betts agreement regarding payment of 6% annually on the capital etc (although the 6% on this capital had actually been paid from its raising).

By the end of 1856, the companies had paid some £541,000 to Peto Brassey & Betts for the construction of the line (the various 'additional works' having of course increased the total). This, plus the money paid to the THD&R Co and minor items, was represented in the 'LT&S' issued capital as follows:-

1852 Act	£400,000	(fully issued)
1854 Act	£50,700	(of the £52,000 authorised)
1856 Act	£42,116	(of the £60,000 authorised)
DEBENTURES		
1852 Act	£100,000	(fully issued)
1856 Act	Nil	(of the £40,000 authorised)
TOTAL ISSUED	£592,816	

(These figures exclude the separate capital for the Gas Factory Junction - Barking branch authorised in 1856 and discussed in chapter 3).

STANFORD-LE-HOPE.   39870.

left
As a result of the flat country, the original LT&S line was burdened with a large number of level crossings. The 1852 Act required that 'a station or a lodge' be erected at all crossings of public roads. At Stanford-le-Hope and Benfleet the crossings seem to have always been looked after by the station staff, but at the other 14 public road crossings 'lodges' to the standard design seen here were provided for resident crossing keepers. These 14 locations were

Tanner Street (Barking)
East Street (Barking)
Rippleside
Mud Island (alias Manor Way, Rainham)
Rainham, Ferry Road
Ordnance Crossing (alias Purfleet Rifle Range)
Purfleet
Manor Road (West Thurrock)
Grays, High Street
Fort Road (Tilbury)
Low Street
Muckingford (alias East Tilbury)
Mucking
Vange (alias Fobbing Crossing)

This view shows Manor Road, looking east towards West Thurrock Junction in 1958. The level crossing here had been replaced for vehicular traffic by an overbridge (from which the photograph was taken) built for access to Hedley's works, so that by this date the cottage was only serving as a residence. In fact, although 10 of the 14 cottages listed survived into the 1950s, the majority had long since only served as staff residences, having been supplanted by signal boxes, or small huts for non-resident keepers, so far as the actual control of the crossing was concerned. Today only one cottage remains standing, at Muckingford, much altered in appearance.

The 'architectural' design of these 1854 cottages makes one wonder if William Tite had any hand in them. Most were brick, but several on marshy ground were timber-built, still with the decorative 'lozenge' in the gable as seen here. Very similar gate cottages appeared on Peto's East Suffolk line of 1859.

It is notable that later LT&S lines avoided level crossings altogether, even though this necessitated in many cases the construction of long approach embankments for roads to take them over the railway.
(Frank Church, courtesy EBEG)

above
Stanford-le-Hope in the Edwardian period. The main building (right) was one of only three of the original 1850s station buildings still extant at 1912. It lasted until burnt down in 1918 (the other two, Purfleet and Thames Haven, lasted into BR days). The down platform shelter at left is also the 1854 original.

The 1852 contract with Peto Brassey & Betts specified that the LT&S stations were to be 'all of the character of the stations on the Northern & Eastern Railway'. However there is no evidence that there was any standard station design on the Stratford-Bishops Stortford section, so one is at a loss to know what this actually meant. Moreover, the original LT&S line stations of 1854-6 were themselves far from standardised. As Tite had been appointed Architect to the LT&SER Committee, the stations ought to have been designed by him, but there is no proof that they were, and they do not particularly bear his mark. All the stations had single-storey main buildings (without stationmaster's house) and a small shelter on the opposite platform.

The two most important intermediate stations, Barking and Grays (see Dow p9 for a view of the latter) had hipped brick buildings with a large overhang on the platform side, on large curved brackets, to give a 'canopy' of sorts. Purfleet had a brick-and-flint building and Stanford-le-Hope this rather 'Brunelian' timber hipped building. Leigh, on a cramped site, was gabled but had the large brackets. Of the original Rainham, Pitsea and Benfleet buildings, no photographs are known. Finally the three termini, Tilbury, Thames Haven, and Southend, were all given timber 'trainshed' roofs; the whole of the buildings at the two former were of timber, necessarily so on the marshy sites, but Southend (Dow p11) received a fairly grand brick building. All in all, a rather random lot!

All the LT&S stations had timber platforms originally. This would have been seen as necessary in some cases due to marshy ground, but in fact it was Peto's standard practice in the 1840s and 1850s to build platforms, underbridges, etc of timber for cheapness. In a report made at the Joint Committee's request in 1859, Bidder and Fowler noted that the timberwork of some of the LT&S platforms and bridges was deteriorating due to its not having been properly, or at all, creosoted. (The Committee might have thought to ask Bidder why, in that case, he had certified the work as satisfactory in 1854!). Accordingly they proposed replacement brick-faced platforms at some stations. The up platform at Stanford-le-Hope was rebuilt in brick, as seen here, but not the down platform. The arrangement of the new brick platform by the station building, where the two gentlemen are standing, is rather horrendous, and it was probably a good job that no Inspecting Officer ever came here after the 1850s! Not only is there a sharp dip downwards, no doubt because the new platform was higher than the old generally but could not be by the doors of the building at this point; there is also a 'hole' at the edge, covered by some sort of moveable plank or trap-door, where wooden steps down to the staff crossing are inset.

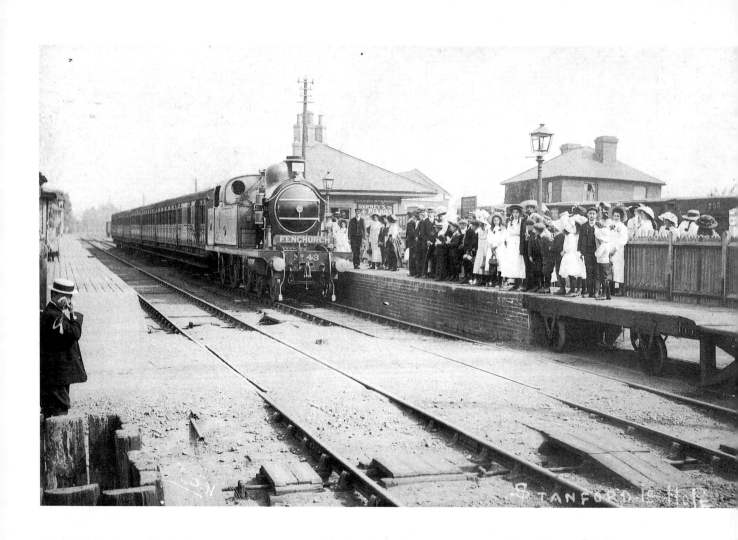

22

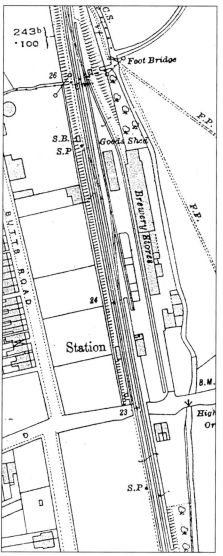

STANFORD-LE-HOPE

Having made Stanford-le-Hope our example in discussing the 1854 stations, it may perhaps be appropriate to note also the subsequent history of the station. This view probably dates from the summer of 1909 as No. 43, arriving with an up train, is in the short-lived lavender grey livery. Some special occasion appears to be depicted and one doubts if there were normally this many passengers joining trains here.

This photograph has been included primarily because it shows well the special feature of the station, the section of 'rolling' platform in the middle of the up platform. When the LT&S line opened the stations all seem to have had only 200ft platforms (except the termini, which needed longer platforms as 'drawing up' was impossible). This was immediately found inadequate on the Barking-Tilbury section and these stations had platform extensions within months of the line opening. But east of Tilbury traffic was lighter and the 200ft platforms at Stanford-le-Hope, Pitsea, Benfleet and Leigh were not extended until 1880/1. This brought a problem with the up platform at Stanford-le-Hope which was sandwiched between the goods yard connections at the north end and the level crossing at the south end. The solution was to build an extra 310ft of platform south of the crossing with this rolling section to link it to the existing platform. When closed the rolling section served as level crossing 'gate' also. (Grays station also had the level crossing in the middle of the platforms from their lengthening in 1854 until the total rebuilding of the station west of the crossing in 1884). The down platform was simply extended at the north end.

The 1915 OS plan shows Stanford-le-Hope in the same form as in the Edwardian photographs. The 1881 signal box at the north end of the down platform was replaced by a new Midland box at the level crossing in 1924. The inner siding in the goods yard was original, the outer siding serving the Brewery Stores dated from c1901. The simple single-storey goods shed (seen in one of the photographs) was a replacement of 1881.

lower left
There is nothing left today of the old Stanford-le-Hope station seen in the previous views. The destruction by fire of the 1854 station building on 1st February 1918 prompted a review of the whole arrangements here which concluded that everything was 'very unsatisfactory'. This resulted in the original section of the up platform north of the crossing being removed around 1920 and the 'rolling' section disposed of; the platform was lengthened at the south end in recompense. New buildings (seen here to the right of the DMU - see also Dow p40 upper, but ignore his caption) were provided on this platform. However the down platform remained north of the crossing until 23.6.1935 when a wholly new down platform was brought into use south of the crossing, opposite the up platform. This April 1958 view shows the station in its 1935 form.

The platforms remain today as in 1935 but a further new building was provided, at the north end of the up platform by the level crossing, on electrification, to meet the needs of the growing town and the c1920 buildings have now been removed.
(Frank Church, courtesy EBEG)

---

below
In the later days of BR operation the Tilbury-Gravesend ferry became an unwanted side-operation, but in the first decades of the line, before the Southend traffic and the London suburban traffic took off, Gravesend was the most important 'station' on the line and the ferry was of vital import. The LT&SR ran boats from the opening of the line and had a monopoly from 1856. The bulk of the traffic was originally London-Gravesend day-trippers, also Gravesend to London residential traffic; but these traffics had faded by the late nineteenth century and the heavy use made of the ferry in the 1880s-1960s period was primarily due to very local work and shopping/entertainment journeys.

The full history of the LT&SR at Tilbury and Gravesend will be featured in a later work. Here, for the present, is TSS Edith on one of her numberless trips, in the early BR years.
(A.Duncan).

PASSENGER TRAIN SERVICES 1854-1858

The Original Services (April 1854)

The line opened with a good service of 11 trains each way, with most trains taking 68 minutes to Tilbury but the faster trains only 50 minutes. All trains had both Bishopsgate and Fenchurch Street portions joined/split at Stratford. Arrival at Gravesend was 10 minutes after Tilbury, making the LT&S service slower to Gravesend than the SER's in most cases. The Sunday service was the same as on weekdays, a reflection of the type of traffic expected, although it is surprising that the full Sunday service was provided in the winter in the 1850s. (Sunday services tended to worsen a little subsequently, and indeed the weekday service of 1854 to Tilbury was sufficiently good that it did not get improved until the 1880s).

Fares

With a cheap fares policy having been consistently intended ever since 1846, the lessees had acquiesced in the inclusion of very low statutory maxima in the 1852 Act - 1d per mile 1st class, 3/4d 2nd, and 1/2d 3rd. (The Act also specified that there should be 3rd Class carriages on at least half the trains). In the event, however, Peto Brassey & Betts quite ignored the Act! - and decided on some very strong 'market pricing', the fares from London being

To Barking Single 1s 0d 1st, 9d 2nd
            Return 1s 8d 1st, 1s 3d 2nd
To all stations beyond including Gravesend
            Single 1s 6d 1st, 1s 0d 2nd
            Return 2s 6d 1st, 1s 8d 2nd

so extracting more from those passengers where the LT&S had a monopoly whilst offering the cheapest possible fares to Gravesend where there was multiple competition. Had any fares been challenged, the lessees would no doubt have responded that the statutory maxima only applied to the LT&S line and not to fares from/to stations west of Forest Gate Junction. However, they also never ran any 3rd class coaches at all during the entire 21 years of the lease! But, thanks to the low fares, everybody was happy and nobody ever sought to dispute the situation.

The SER's fares to Gravesend were twice the LT&S', although they did have 'Excursion' returns at the same price as the LT&S returns, valid for specific trains only.

The 1852 Agreement provided that the lessees should pay over to the L&BR and ECR one-third of the gross passenger fare to Tilbury/Gravesend and intermediate stations, and one-quarter for stations beyond Tilbury; this payment to be divided between the two companies in proportion to mileage (the ECR getting the whole for passengers from Bishopsgate, and the L&BR and ECR sharing by mileage for passengers from Fenchurch Street). These sums included 'terminal' charges. The payments became regarded as exorbitant (see Chapter 3).

Opening to Southend

The service to Stanford-le-Hope from August 1854 was provided by extending 4 down and 5 up trains (reduced to 3 down and 4 up in the winter).

On opening to Leigh in July 1855, there were 4 trains each way beyond Tilbury (8.7, 10.37. 4.22 and 7.7 from Fenchurch Street; and 7.55, 10.50, 4.40, and 6.50 from Leigh).

The opening to Southend in March 1856 initially brought a reduction to 3 trains each way beyond Tilbury, this being blamed on the Board of Trade's restrictions on the use of the single line. The service was increased to 5 when the line was doubled in May, then to 6 in June, reducing to 4 in the winter of 1856/7. (Indeed in some of the following winters it sank to 3 again).

The fares to Southend were set at a higher level (although still low by national standards)
3s 6d 1st, 2s 6d 2nd Single
5s 10d 1st, 4s 2d 2nd Return

Withdrawal of Bishopsgate portions (1856)

It was found that, thanks to the more convenient site of Fenchurch Street, most LT&S passengers preferred it to Bishopsgate. In the year 1855, 757,811 LT&S passengers used Fenchurch Street, and only 196,527 Bishopsgate. As a result many trains lost their Bishopsgate portions during 1856, and finally from 1.11.1856 all Bishopsgate portions ceased. From this time on 'LT&S' trains were wholly Fenchurch Street-based. The ECR was of course still receiving 'mileage' for the use of the Bow Junction to Forest Gate Junction section.

Bradshaw Timetable for June 1854 (the first month the LT&S line appears in Bradshaw). There are probably two errors in the printing; the omission of the Bishopsgate portion of the 8.7pm down and the omission of the intermediate stops in the 11.40am up. Note the regular departure slots at xx07, xx22 and xx37 from Fenchurch Street, a necessity to fit in with the other services from that station (Blackwall trains at xx00, xx15, xx30, xx45; North London trains at xx05, xx20, xx35, xx50; and 'Woolwich' trains at xx25 and xx55). How the LT&S trains could leave only 2 minutes behind the NLR trains on a line whose signalmen were instructed, under the usual 'time-interval' rules of the period, to show a 'stop' signal for 5 minutes after a train had passed, must remain a secret known only to the L&BR's management! - but it continued so for years. The non-stopping at Barking and Grays, the most important places on the line after Gravesend, was not to last long.

LONDON, TILBURY, and SOUTHEND.

Bradshaw Timetable for November 1856. There are 10 trains each way on the London-Tilbury section in this winter service, with 2½ hour gaps in the middle of the day. The ECR services between Bishopsgate and Stratford not being all that frequent at this date, there are several trains which do not even have connections to/from Bishopsgate now that the through coaches have been withdrawn. All trains now call at Barking and Grays. The Gravesend connections are shown in full here. In the early years two boats connected with most trains, one from Rosherville Pier and one from the Town Pier, but the Rosherville sailings were soon cut back and ceased altogether in 1900. The extension of the Town Pier boats to/from the Terrace Pier was only done briefly in 1856/8.

CHAPTER 3

The Lessees' Railway (1854-1875)

For the first half of Peto Brassey & Betts' 21-year lease, the LT&S was at the centre of an on-off conflict between Peto and the ECR. But the formation of the GER in 1862 (and its absorption of the L&BR in 1865) which put an end to Peto's territorial machinations in East Anglia, followed by Peto's bankruptcy, meant that the last half of the lease merely dragged on without any positive interest in the line on the lessees' part. Another factor through this period was the increasing demand of the almost-impotent LT&S shareholders to gain some influence in the running of their railway.

THE ECR SHAREHOLDERS' REVOLT (1855)

From March 1851 Peto's friend David Waddington had been the leading figure in the ECR as Chairman. But by 1855 many of the ECR shareholders were becoming restive at his methods, and his relationship with Peto in particular. In July 1855 the shareholders voted against a proposed ECR working agreement for Peto's East Suffolk Railway (for more on which see later), which they saw as another Peto-Waddington plot at their expense. Then in August 1855 the ECR half-yearly meeting appointed a 'Committee of Investigation' under Horatio Love. Their report was published in November and had much to say about the LT&S line working agreement, which it described as 'utterly astonishing, of which the shareholders must form their own conclusions'. The ECR was receiving an income of only £400 pa to cover the £47,159 spent on stock for the LT&S line - not even enough to cover the depreciation. 'We do not hesitate to say that there is grave cause for suspicion as to the nature of the relations between Mr Waddington and Messrs Peto Brassey & Betts', noted the *Daily News* on 1st December. *The Railway Times* on 7th December had a leader entitled 'THE TILBURY JOB'. But the LT&S was only one worm in the can that the Committee uncovered. The press was full of ECR scandals for months afterwards and there were many riotous shareholders' meetings.

(In 1861, when they were entitled to a seven-year review of the 1854 working agreement, the ECR got the lessees to agree to the charge for locomotive power for passenger trains being increased from 8d to 8½d per mile, and for goods trains from 10d to 1s per mile).

It became clear that the anti-Waddington forces were going to seek to have him expelled at the February 1856 ECR half-yearly meeting. As part of the Waddington camp's scheming to prevent this, Peto Brassey Betts and Bidder bought up enormous numbers of ECR shares themselves. This was enough to get Waddington re-elected for the moment, but his position was clearly under doubt.

THE 'BARKING BRANCH'

It was hardly to be regarded as coincidence that on 9th October 1855, at the very time when the ECR Investigation Committee's discoveries were becoming known, Peto went to the LT&S Joint Committee to seek approval for a new line, always referred to at this promotional period as the 'Barking Branch', from Gas Factory Junction* on the L&BR to the existing LT&S line at Barking West Junction. The 'public' purpose of this line was the need to get LT&S trains away from the increasing congestion on the ECR at Stratford; however, it also just happened to enable 'LT&S' trains running from Fenchurch Street to avoid ECR metals altogether! - a great benefit to Messrs Peto Brassey & Betts should a post-Waddington ECR turn against them. Of course, this Gas Factory Junction - Barking line was no new idea; it had been part of the L&BR's scheme of 1851 during the last period of hostility from the ECR, and indeed went back to the L&BR's 1846 'London & South Essex Railway' in a still earlier period of ECR hostility. It must have always been present

as a possibility in Peto's mind, for pulling out of the drawer again at any time that his relations with the ECR went sour.

Having said all that, the congestion at Stratford was also a real problem. In the summer 1855 timetable there were 113 passenger and about 18 goods trains daily over the Bow-Stratford section, with many conflicting movements at Stratford. Wightman the LT&S line Manager told the 1856 House of Commons committee that an analysis of guards' journals showed that in the previous year there had been 506 cases of LT&S trains being detained more than 10 minutes at Stratford (about 6% of the total LT&S trains), and that 'we very frequently have occasion to complain'.

On 18th October 1855 Bidder attended the ECR Board to put the scheme to them formally. They agreed, but at a high price - that 'the traffic which passes over the deviation line will be considered as passing over the existing line', ie that the ECR would still get mileage payments for the Bow-Forest Gate section even though the 'LT&S' trains would no longer actually run over this section at all! Full details were hammered out at a special ECR Board on 13th November where John Hawkshaw, who was to be appointed as 'Arbitrator' under the Act to settle any differences that might arise from this arrangement subsequently, was present as a 'neutral' adviser. Peto also agreed with the L&BR that they would get a half-share of the fares from Fenchurch Street to the stations on the new line (Bromley, Plaistow and East Ham).

In addition to the main Gas Factory Junction - Barking line, there were two spurs proposed at Abbey Mills to the ECR's North Woolwich line. The south curve was intended for use by the ECR's Fenchurch Street - North Woolwich service, enabling these trains also to avoid the Stratford congestion and giving them a generally shorter route. The north curve was for the ECR's Woodford & Loughton line trains (this line was then nearing completion, and opened in August 1856); it will be recalled that it had previously been agreed with the L&BR that the bulk of the trains off this line would run to Fenchurch Street, and by means of this Abbey Mills north curve they would be able to run via Stratford Low Level and so also avoid the Stratford congestion. (In the event the north curve never materialised, and they actually ran via Stratford main line and Bow Junction). In November 1855 it was agreed that the Abbey Mills north and south curves would be built as purely ECR lines (rather than 'LT&S' ECR/L&BR Joint), which was reasonable enough given that only ECR trains would use them. However it was subsequently agreed that they would be 'LT&S' instead and they were so authorised in the Act. The fact that the ECR would itself benefit, via these curves, from the building of the 'Barking Branch' was no doubt an important reason in their not opposing it.

However, despite the ECR's agreement, Peto was clearly concerned at the volatile situation on the ECR, and in case they should turn hostile before the Act was obtained and succeed in getting the 'LT&S' Bill for the line withdrawn, Peto Brassey & Betts in combination with the L&BR Board also promoted a Bill for an identical line themselves under the name of the 'London Barking & Victoria Docks Junction Railway'. (This name points to another advantage of these lines to Peto Brassey & Betts, namely that it would enable the goods traffic from their Victoria Dock, opened November 1855, to reach an as-yet-unbuilt

---

* *Although the name 'Gas Factory Junction' is used throughout here, and had certainly been in use for the NLR line junction since its opening in 1850, it appears that the LT&S line junction was actually known as 'Bromley Junction' from 1858 to 1869 and regarded as a 'separate location'. However, when an interlocked signal box was built at the NLR junction in 1869, the LT&S line points were moved south to the NLR junction so that they too could be worked from this box, with gauntletted tracks from there to the route junction. This made the LT&S junction part of 'Gas Factory Junction'. The gauntletting was abolished in 1886 when a replacement box was opened.*

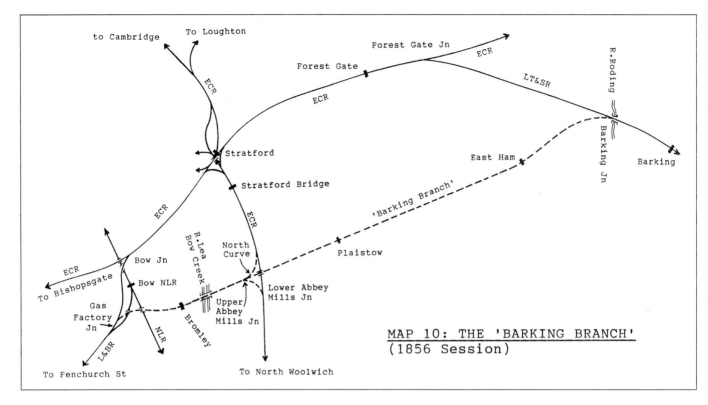

MAP 10: THE 'BARKING BRANCH'
(1856 Session)

goods station for central London on the L&BR line near Fenchurch Street, without touching the ECR main line). The *Railway Times* noted that the L&BR Directors, Bidder and Fowler had put down for most of the shares in this nebulous 'LB&VDJR' themselves! In the event, however, the ECR situation was salvaged for the period of the parliamentary proceedings on the 'LT&S' Bill for the line, and the LB&VDJR Bill was accordingly withdrawn before its parliamentary consideration began.

There being no other parties with cause to oppose the 'LT&S' Bill for the line, it went through Parliament without difficulty, and was authorised by the London Tilbury & Southend Railway (Extension & Branches) Act 1856, receiving the Royal Assent on 7th July 1856. An additional share capital of £150,000 and additional borrowing of £50,000 were authorised to finance the line, which was to be owned by the ECR and L&BR jointly in the same way as the existing LT&S line, forming an integral part of the LT&S 'undertaking'.

On 16th April the Joint Committee had approved a contract with Peto Brassey & Betts for the building of the line at £200,000 on the same basis as for the previous capital i.e. they to pay 6% on the share capital and the 4% on the debentures, the new line to be incorporated within the lease from opening. The additional agreement with Peto Brassey & Betts for this was dated 1st July 1856 but not sealed until after the Act was

passed.

Construction of the line began shortly afterwards, without any serious hold-ups. The main features were a 41-arch brick viaduct from Gas Factory Junction to Campbell Road (incorporating a bridge over the NLR curve up to Gas Factory Junction); the 137ft-span bridge over the NLR Poplar line, which was so lengthy because the NLR Bow Works sidings were also crossed; the bridges over the River Lea and Bow Creek; and the bridge over the ECR North Woolwich line. The new line joined the existing LT&S line at the west side of the River Roding bridge, so avoiding an additional bridge here. Except for the first short stretch on the viaduct, the line passed through open fields and no property demolition was necessary (Bromley and Plaistow were becoming built up, but not on the line chosen).

An Engineers' report from Bidder and Fowler on 13th August 1857 noted that all land was now in the contractors' hands except for half a mile at East Ham, four and a half miles of single line had been laid, and the stations would shortly be commenced. The brick viaduct was nearly complete, the main NLR bridge was awaiting delivery of the girders and 76 of the 90 piles for the adjacent Lea and Bow Creek bridges were driven. From there to Plaistow the embankment was nearing completion and would be finished in 6 weeks. The Abbey Mills curves were not yet commenced. In the cutting between Plaistow and East Ham three of the seven overbridges were completed and in

The 1858 LT&SR bridge over the NLR Poplar line, shortly before it was replaced. The photographer is looking north with the NLR running lines at left; the lines on the right are all dead-end sidings to the Bow Works buildings seen in the background.

This bridge was replaced by a new one on the same alignment in 1904.

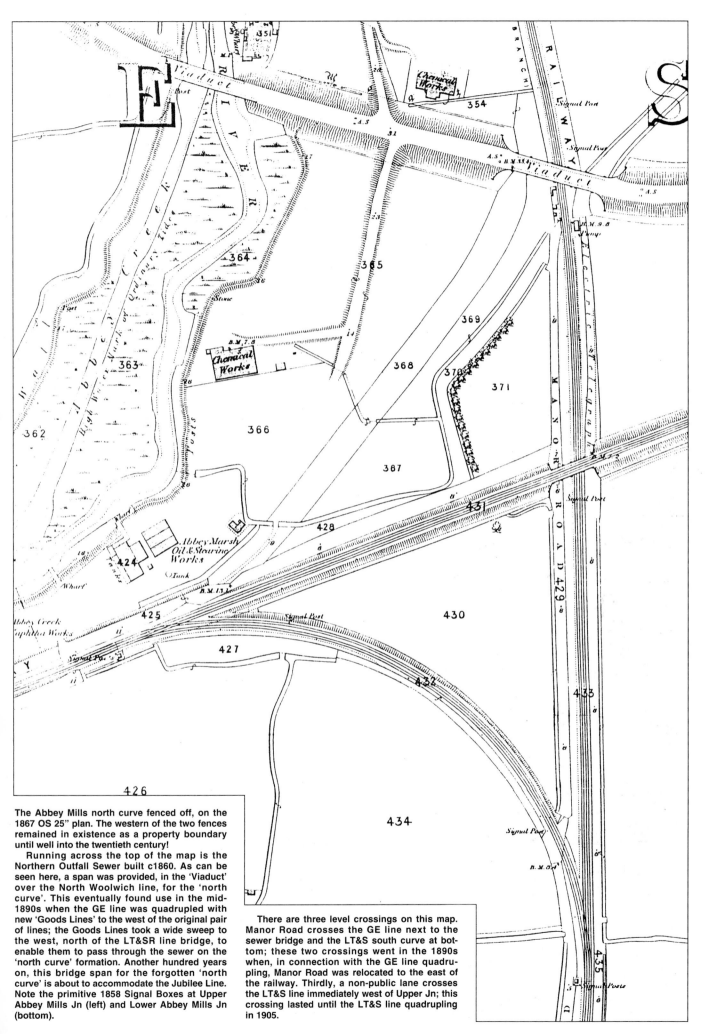

The Abbey Mills north curve fenced off, on the 1867 OS 25" plan. The western of the two fences remained in existence as a property boundary until well into the twentieth century!

Running across the top of the map is the Northern Outfall Sewer built c1860. As can be seen here, a span was provided, in the 'Viaduct' over the North Woolwich line, for the 'north curve'. This eventually found use in the mid-1890s when the GE line was quadrupled with new 'Goods Lines' to the west of the original pair of lines; the Goods Lines took a wide sweep to the west, north of the LT&SR line bridge, to enable them to pass through the sewer on the 'north curve' formation. Another hundred years on, this bridge span for the forgotten 'north curve' is about to accommodate the Jubilee Line. Note the primitive 1858 Signal Boxes at Upper Abbey Mills Jn (left) and Lower Abbey Mills Jn (bottom).

There are three level crossings on this map. Manor Road crosses the GE line next to the sewer bridge and the LT&S south curve at bottom; these two crossings went in the 1890s when, in connection with the GE line quadrupling, Manor Road was relocated to the east of the railway. Thirdly, a non-public lane crosses the LT&S line immediately west of Upper Jn; this crossing lasted until the LT&S line quadrupling in 1905.

use, two were in progress and two not yet begun. The embankment from East Ham to Barking was completed and ballasted.When the Lea and Bow Creek bridges were finished, 'cut' would be taken from the cutting west of East Ham for use in making the embankments between Campbell Road and the Lea.

The next report on 26th February 1858 stated that Bromley and East Ham stations would be finished in about six weeks, and that the line might be opened about 'the middle or latter end of April'. The Abbey Mills south curve was now complete, as on 3rd March Sinclair the ECR Engineer told the ECR Traffic Committee that the contractors were now waiting to put in the junction on the North Woolwich line, which was approved. The previous day the L&BR had ordered the pointwork for the Gas Factory Junction.

Somewhat unusually, it proved possible to open the line before the Engineer's predicted date. The Board of Trade inspection was made by Capt Tyler who reported favourably on 27th March and the line opened without ceremony on 31st March 1858. All 'LT&S' passenger trains were diverted over the new line from that date, the ECR beginning a Bishopsgate-Barking service to maintain a service over the Forest Gate-Barking section. As with previous LT&S line openings, it is not specifically known that goods traffic at Plaistow (not Bromley and East Ham, which did not handle goods until much later) also began on this date; we have to assume that it did, but how it was dealt with is not known, as the main LT&S goods services ran via Stratford until 1876.

The Abbey Mills south curve also seems to have 'opened' on 31.3.1858, but there is no known evidence of booked traffic until 1st June 1858* when many of the ECR Fenchurch Street-North Woolwich passenger trains were diverted via Bromley, as

had been intended. Interestingly the LT&SR 1856 Act had actually given the ECR running powers over the Gas Factory Junction - Upper Abbey Mills Junction - Lower Abbey Mills Junction sections of the new line, a rather odd provision given that the ECR was joint owner of it! - although one for which the GER was no doubt grateful later. It was almost as though the LT&S was already becoming seen as something 'separate' from its owners. The Abbey Mills south curve, although part of the LT&S system, was never to be served by any LT&SR (or its successors) train service - indeed it could not be because they had no running powers over the North Woolwich line beyond - but only by the trains of the ECR and successors.

The Abbey Mills north curve was never built at all, although the land was fenced off ready for work to start. After six years the GER Traffic Committee decided in January 1864 that it should now be built, and asked Bidder to see Wightman about it. Nothing further is then heard until April 1865 when the GER officers were asked to report on it, but the subject then became muddled with a possible GER takeover of the LT&SR (discussed later) and then got forgotten when that came to nought. In 1874 Kennell somewhat belatedly reminded the Joint Committee that the 1856 Act had specified that if the north curve were not completed by 1860, no dividends could be paid to LT&S shareholders thereafter! This, after being duly ignored all these years, was rectified by the LT&SR 1875 Act which authorised the abandonment of the north curve.

There was no booked goods traffic in 1858; the goods trains run by the ECR/GER on behalf of Peto Brassey & Betts (later the London & St Katharine Dock Co) from Mint St (later Goodmans Yard) to the Victoria Dock did not begin until 1.8.1858, and in any case ran via Stratford Western Junction until 1877 when they began running via Bromley and the Abbey Mills curve.

The Abbey Mills of later years, looking west from West Ham LT&SR station in May 1932. In the foreground are the bridges over both Manor Road and the North Woolwich line. The double track bridge at centre is on the line of the original 1858 bridge, the two single-track bridges either side date from the 1905 LT&SR quadrupling. However at Upper Abbey Mills Junction (seen in the distance, with the signal box on the up side) the 1905 quadrupling was done wholly on the up side, hence the 'slew' clearly seen in this view with all four lines shifting to the south. The 1/100 down gradient is also clear.

The sidings and depot at left, connected to the LT&S line at Upper Junction, were put in for the London & Thames Haven Oil Wharves Ltd, who brought oil here from Thames Haven, in 1880 and lasted until 1937. The embankment of the 'south curve' is beyond.

From the 1860s the Abbey Mills marshes were colonised by chemical works and other offensive and polluting industries. They were being forced out of inner London and settled here because the West Ham authorities took little control. The marshes were unsuitable for housing development.
(D. J. Taylor collection)

PETO vs THE ECR: THE TILBURY, MALDON & COLCHESTER RAILWAY (1856-7)

Waddington's position as ECR Chairman became steadily less tenable during 1856, and on 10th July, a mere three days after the Act for the 'Barking branch' was passed, he was obliged to announce that he was resigning. A few months later Horatio Love, the former Chairman of the Investigatory Committee, succeeded to the ECR company chairmanship. He was no friend of Bidder and Peto.

With the ECR now hostile again, Peto launched an out-and-out attack on them in the autumn of 1856 in the form of the 'Tilbury Maldon & Colchester Railway'. The politics of this scheme were somewhat complex, but basically it arose from Peto's Lowestoft interests and his wish to have Lowestoft-London traffic routed via his East Suffolk Railway (Act 1854) instead of via Norwich, a prospect which the post-Waddington ECR disliked. The TM&CR was meant to serve as a gun held at the ECR's head to force them to work the East Suffolk as Peto wanted (in which case the TM&CR would be dropped), or alternatively as part of a new Peto-controlled through route, if the ECR remained obstinate. It actually involved a line from Pitsea to Colchester, with a branch to Burnham-on-Crouch thrown in for good measure.

The scheme first became public at a meeting between Peto and Colchester Town Council on 24th September 1856. A week later Peto was dining with the burghers of Yarmouth, and told them that 'he should not be satisfied till he had what was equivalent to an independent route from Yarmouth to London, if the ECR obstructed the East Suffolk traffic' - meaning, one imagines, that he would promote if necessary a parallel line to the ECR's from Woodbridge to Colchester and so continue via the TM&CR and the LT&SR (including the so-convenient 'Barking branch') and so reach Fenchurch Street without touching the ECR anywhere. The TM&CR would also of course benefit Peto's pocket by increasing the traffic on the LT&S.

The TM&CR plans (by Fowler) were deposited in November 1856. The L&BR were thoroughly mixed up in it all, and Kennell was appointed Secretary to the TM&CR. Peto claimed that £596,750 of the £700,000 capital had already been subscribed, but a blistering attack from the *Railway Times* in January noted that £584,000 of this had been put down for by Peto Brassey and Betts themselves, the L&BR's Directors and officers, and various financiers involved with them. The TM&CR's 'Provisional Directors' were however all 'local gents' including the Mayors of Gravesend, Maldon and Colchester. They were all appointed in a rush in the days before the prospectus was published on 10th December and Peto assured them that they would not be liable for anything financially!

The ECR naturally reacted by promoting 'blocking lines' from Shenfield to Pitsea, Pitsea to Maldon and a branch of their own to the Crouch.

The TM&CR did attract some local support, not least in Colchester where many disliked the ECR train service and the inconvenient position of the station (Peto was promising them a 'central station', and a journey time of only one and a half hours to Fenchurch Street by express train despite the circuitous route). A public meeting in Colchester on 26th December produced a unanimous motion for, although one voice did venture to suggest that the TM&CR was 'not a bona fide undertaking'.

The owner of the *Railway Times,* Norris, was an ECR director, and he therefore enjoyed himself in the early part of 1857 attacking Peto's eminently-attackable scheme, and giving free rein to a correspondent signing himself as 'A Tooth of the Dragon' who did the same at great length. They referred to the LT&S as 'a vampire eating the life-blood of the Eastern Counties' (a reference to the working agreement). Peto, they said, was no doubt intending to make a good profit by contracting to build the line himself at an excessive sum, just as he had done with the LT&S line.

In the event, the parliamentary contest between the TM&CR and the rival ECR proposals never came off. In late April Brassey (probably because he was seen as a less insufferable figure than Peto himself!) had talks with Love on the subject, and a special ECR Board meeting was held on 8th April 1857 at which Brassey put forward 'Heads of Agreement' including

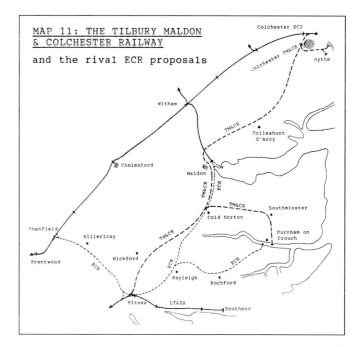

MAP 11: THE TILBURY MALDON & COLCHESTER RAILWAY

and the rival ECR proposals

extremely detailed proposals for the future split of Yarmouth and Lowestoft revenue after the East Suffolk line opened, all on the basis that Peto would withdraw the TM&CR scheme and the ECR would agree to work the East Suffolk (and also of course that the ECR would withdraw their now wholly pointless rival plans). This was agreed, and made public in *The Times* on 9th April.

The LT&S line, therefore, never saw any trains from Colchester or Lowestoft. This was really the end of Peto's machinations in East Anglia, although there were one or two hitches before the East Suffolk agreement was formally concluded in the summer of 1858, and the ECR became worried from time to time that Peto might get involved in various schemes, promoted by Eastern Union and Norfolk Railway interests in 1858-61, for lines from the LT&S at Barking West Junction to Bury St Edmunds to give those companies independent access to London free of the ECR. In fact Peto kept out of these and they were in any case finally defeated by the ECR's 'block lines' (Bishops Stortford-Braintree, Sudbury-Shelford and Long Melford-Bury) authorised in 1861.

In August 1862 the Eastern Union, Norfolk, and East Suffolk were fully merged with the Eastern Counties under the name of the new Great Eastern Railway, with Love as Chairman, bringing stability at last to the previously so volatile East Anglian railway scene.

INDEPENDENT SCHEMES IN SOUTH ESSEX

The schemes promoted by the L&BR and Peto in the 1840s and '50s had offered hopes of railway communication to various communities in the area between the LT&SR line and the ECR Colchester line. When these came to nought it was natural that independent initiatives should spring up to fill these gaps. None of these came at all close to success, but it may be of interest to note briefly those which would have involved connection with the LT&SR line.

The **Southend & Burnham Railway** of 1857/8 proposed a line from the LT&SR at Southend to a pier on the Crouch opposite Burnham-on-Crouch. Plans were deposited but no Bill was lodged.

The **South Essex Railway** actually obtained two Acts, one in 1865 for a Shenfield-Billericay-Wickford-Southminster line with a branch to Maldon and the second in 1866 for a line from the LT&SR at Pitsea to join the 1865 line east of Wickford. Peto sought to oppose the 1865 Bill on the grounds that it would take away the Wickford traffic currently handled by the LT&SR at Pitsea station, but the LT&SR Board did not consider the expense of opposition worthwhile. The promoters, of whom the engineer G.W. Hemans seems to have been foremost, secured the GER's agreement to working the line, but the GER never translated its moral support into hard financial support. The 'SER', in the usual way, faded into non-existence after a few years, and was formally wound up in 1874.

The **Rochford Hundred Railway,** which appears to have had different promoters to the 'SER', deposited plans in 1866 for a line from the 'SER' at Wickford to Rayleigh, Rochford and Southend (so that the two schemes together would have formed a route similar to the GER line of the 1880s). However the scheme was not proceeded with in parliament.

The **Billericay Railway** was floated in the 1869-71 period for a Brentwood-Billericay-Pitsea line to supplant the moribund 'SER', but the GER would not become involved, and no plans were ever drawn up.

The **Southend & Shoeburyness Railway** deposited plans in 1868 but did no more.

The **Southend & Maldon Railway** deposited in 1871, was to have run from the LT&SR at Southend to the GER at Maldon, via Rochford and Fambridge. The scheme was deposited again in 1878 as the **East & South Essex Railway** and lingered until 1881.

The last independent initiative, before the LT&SR and the GER eventually filled in the gaps on the map themselves in the 1880s, was another **Southend & Shoeburyness Railway** in 1881.

THE LT&SR BECOMES A COMPANY (1862)

1862 also saw the first step in the peculiar course of events that was to end in the LT&SR becoming a rival company to the GER, after having been initially the joint property of two of the GER's constituents.

The LT&SR Act 1862, which constituted the LT&SR as a separate company instead of a jointly-owned undertaking, was effectively promoted by the lessees with the aim of making it easier for them to escape from the existing lease,on which they were losing money. However most of the shareholders were in the dark about this at the time, and approved the Bill because the incorporation of the LT&SR as a company gave them the chance to have a partial say in the direction for the first time.

The matter was initiated early in November 1861 when a meeting of 'several of the principle shareholders' was held at William Tite's office, and a resolution was passed that a Bill should be promoted to turn the LT&SR into a company. A 'Committee of Shareholders' was appointed to deal with this, comprising

> William Tite
> Jacob G. Cope
> Sydney Lawrence
> Thomson Hankey
> Thomas Vardon

of whom the first three at least were known Peto associates (indeed, Lawrence was Peto's stockbroker). The Committee immediately approached the Joint Committee, and met them on 9th November. The Joint Committee, perhaps not surprisingly, were not enamoured of this attempt by their child to leave home. But because of the peculiar constitution of the LT&S, under which the railway companies themselves did not hold any shares in 'their' property, the Joint Committee could not control the matter. At an Extraordinary shareholders' meeting on 17th December a motion for was carried by a large majority - strongly opposed by Love, who no doubt was better informed than many.

The Bill was not opposed in parliament by the ECR or L&BR, and the Act was passed on 16th May 1862. The 'undertaking of the London Tilbury and Southend Extension Railway' (sic) was 'vested' in the new London Tilbury and Southend Railway Company. The Joint Committee became the company Board. The Act provided for nine Directors, of whom three were to be elected by the ECR, three by the L&BR, and three by the shareholders.

The ECR appointed Love, George Palmer and Samuel Anderson; the L&BR Daniell, Wilson and Bishop (who had all been on the Joint Committee ever since 1852); and the shareholders (on Tite's proposal) Cope, Lawrence, and Vardon. One speaker ventured to object to Lawrence in view of his position as Peto's broker.

Otherwise there was little change; Daniell remained Chairman, Kennell was formally appointed Secretary to the new company, and Bidder and Fowler remained the Engineers.

The *Railway Times* noted:- 'The holders of shares in this undertaking, leased to one party and worked by another, having obtained their Act of Incorporation, are somewhat at a loss as to what to do with it. They cannot control the traffic; they need not to interfere with the expenses; and there cannot be the slightest vestige of hope, so long as the earnings (are) little more than 3% on the outlay, of any surplus above their guarantee of 6% coming to them'.

However, by December 1862 the same journal was able to point out 'The purpose of incorporating the shareholders in this undertaking is becoming more and more evident. The immediate object is for (Peto) to get rid of the lease prior to its legal termination in 1875'.

THE 1863 ACT AND THE PROPOSED 4½% LEASE TO THE GER AND L&BR

The LT&SR Act 1863, which received the Royal Assent on 22nd June 1863, was promoted by the lessees to authorise alterations in the terms of the lease, the ending of the lease, the arranging of a new lease to the GER and L&BR instead, and various other possible revised arrangements. It was only an enabling Act and did not require anything to be done at all. There was no opposition to the Bill in parliament.

Brassey had attended the GER Board in November 1862 to discuss possible 'alterations of the guarantee to the shareholders', and Love had further meetings with Peto and Brassey after this. However, at the February 1863 half-yearly shareholders' meeting the LT&SR Board professed themselves ignorant of why the Bill was being promoted!

As the 1854 Act merely *enabled* the granting of a lease to Peto Brassey & Betts for *up to* 21 years, it is not actually clear why it was deemed necessary to seek specific legislative authority now to amend or end it.

It soon became known that the course favoured by the lessees was a 999-year lease of the LT&SR to the GER and L&BR jointly, with the two companies guaranteeing 4½% annually to the shareholders, and Peto Brassey & Betts undertaking to pay any difference annually between the actual earnings of the line and 4½% (so that the two companies would be protected against the possibility of having to run the line at a loss - this to apply up to 1875 only, however). Peto and Brassey put this scheme to the LT&SR Board on 30th June 1863 and it was agreed by the GER and L&BR Boards on 7th July.

The benefits of the scheme to Peto Brassey & Betts were obvious enough - they would be ensured a saving of at least the 1½% per annum, a reduction of their annual loss on the line to about half what it was under the existing arrangements. The GER and L&BR could not lose financially and would be able to get their errant child back in the fold (it might be noted, of course, that prior to the 1862 Act it would not have been necessary to arrange a lease of the LT&SR to the GER and L&BR if the Peto Brassey & Betts lease came to an end, because they had up to then owned it anyway!). What was more debatable was how the scheme could be sold to the shareholders. The argument adopted was that a 4½% guarantee from established railway companies was a more solid thing than 6% guaranteed by private persons, and that this would serve to raise the market value of LT&SR stock (which had in fact risen from 87 to 100 in the first half of 1863 on the basis of speculation on the likely changes after the Act).

A special LT&SR shareholders' meeting was held on 28th July 1863, the threat of reduced dividends bringing a large attendance. Tite and Bidder made lengthy speeches for the proposal. But very few were convinced, and the Board did not dare to ask for a vote. The meeting then appointed a shareholders' committee to confer with the Directors on the matter pending another full meeting in three weeks time. This committee comprised Charles Eley and Thomas Moxon, who had been leading voices against the proposal at the meeting, Tite, and two others. They produced a majority report against the proposal (Tite of course being in the minority).

Following the July meeting, Peto Brassey and Betts then set to work to use various dubious tactics to try to ensure the approval of the scheme at the resumed meeting. They split up most of the large shareholdings held by their allies into multiple smaller holdings, which would benefit them at a vote as the large holdings carried proportionately less representation than a smaller holding. No less than 136 transfers were sent to the Registrar in this three week period. (In November Brassey claimed that he alone was responsible for all this and that Peto and Betts had known nothing of it, but it is doubtful if anyone believed this). Secondly, they got people to start spreading rumours about their financial position, with the idea that this would bring support for a 'reliable' 4½% rather than a 'dubious' 6%. And thirdly, they arranged that the date and time of the resumed meeting were only announced two days in advance to the ordinary shareholders, whilst making sure at the same time that all the 'shadow shareholders', into whose names stock had been temporarily transferred by them, were present at the meeting to vote for the proposal.

These ploys however all failed. Eley and Moxon were able, at great effort, to get ordinary proprietors to the resumed meeting on 18th August in large numbers.

The 'share-splitting' tactic was made public before the meeting, and when it became clear that the proposal would be lost, the programmed 'supporters' were met on the landing outside the meeting room and sent away as 'their presence would be inconvenient'. The meeting began with Samuel Anderson, who was in the chair in Daniell's absence, reading a letter from Brassey announcing that the proposal had been withdrawn owing to the adverse reaction to it. Anderson and the rest of the Board then immediately left the room declaring the meeting at an end, so that no questions could be asked. However the shareholders elected Moxon to the chair and the meeting resumed with Eley reading the committee's majority report, and then attacking Tite and various members of the Board. A resolution was passed that the report be circulated to all shareholders.

So came to nothing yet another course of events that might have seen the LT&SR becoming part of the GER.

The real significance of these events of 1863 in retrospect was that the ordinary holders of LT&SR stock - those not associated with Peto Brassey & Betts and the old ECR influences - had found a voice for the first time. One of them wrote to the *Railway Times* at the end of August:- 'Up to a very recent period we have been like obedient children, doing just as we were bid. Our friend Mr Tite has done exactly what he pleased with us'.

A special general meeting on 24th November 1863 resolved to appoint a 'Committee of Investigation' - shades of the ECR! - to report to the shareholders on all questions. This Committee was comprised of Eley, Moxon, and four others - but not Tite or any of his friends, whose day was coming to an end.

THE INVESTIGATORY COMMITTEE'S REPORT (1864)

The Committee's report, which told the full tale of the events of 1862/3 publicly for the first time, was read to and approved by the next half-yearly shareholders' meeting on 23rd February 1864. (The Board also produced a counter-report, but little notice was taken of this). The main thrust of the Committee's argument was that the line could never expect to produce more than 6% under the present lease, due to the heavy tolls paid to the L&BR and ECR by the lessees; but that the long term traffic and revenue prospects - the tolls were renegotiable at the end of the lease - were much better, and the shareholders should not therefore be tempted by any low offer now, but should be content with their 6% until 1875 and hope for better things thereafter. (In many ways this was the right analysis, although the general fall-off in British railway dividends subsequently was to mean that the LT&SR never actually paid more than 5-6%).

The report is useful to us in that it gives a good picture of the LT&SR's situation in the middle of the lessees' period, for which information is otherwise on the scarce side.

Of the tolls the Committee said 'It is conceded by everybody that these tolls are of a most exorbitant nature; they would not have been submitted to by the lessees, only that, anxious to secure the anticipated profit on the contract, they were obliged to make the concession as the price to be paid to the two companies for their co-operation'.

Full figures were given for the 12 months ending 30.6.1853 to show the effect of the tolls on the profits:-

GROSS RECEIPTS	Passenger	£71,653
	Goods	£11,267
	Total	£82,920

of which £82,920, a sum of £24,810 was paid over to the other companies as follows:-

L&BR	Passenger	£12,280
	Goods	£ 1,855
GER	Passenger	£7,336
	Goods	£1,634
NLR	Passenger	£1,545
	Goods	£161
		£24,810

(the 'goods' payments were based on a 'normal' mileage and terminal basis, not on the special arrangements under the 1852 Agreement with the lessees that covered the 'passenger' tolls).

The NET RECEIPTS were therefore £58,111.

The working expenses were £35,219. (The Committee thought this on the high side, at 60.6%, given that companies were regularly working others for 50% elsewhere, and that the LT&S line ought to be unusually cheap to maintain. They noted that the maintenance was done by the lessees at their own prices).

Hence the PROFITS for the 12 months were £22,892.

The sum paid by the lessees to the proprietors (at 6% on the approx £650,000 capital and 4% on the approx £150,000 debentures) was around £45,000 per annum, thus giving the lessees a loss of around £22,000 (which ties in with Brassey's statement at the November 1863 meeting that they were losing £24,000 a year).

Passenger figures were (counting return journeys as 2 and ignoring the 413 Season Ticket holders), for the 12 months:-

To/From Fenchurch Street and Stepney	1,012,996	£54,674
To/From Bishopsgate and GER	41,029	£2,956
To/From NLR	131,067	£6,326
Local Traffic between LT&S stations	270,852	£7,697
	1,455,944	£71,653

(this again shows the insignificance of the Bishopsgate traffic).

If we sit back and consider the 'tolls' from a neutral viewpoint, the Committee were perhaps over-painting a little. The *original* tolls under which the two companies took a third of the gross fare for stations to Tilbury, and a quarter for stations beyond Tilbury, were not so unreasonable given that 'terminals' for the use of Fenchurch Street and Bishopsgate stations were included. Indeed for stations Barking to Purfleet the third share was less than a mileage proportion. For Tilbury, which had the greatest traffic originally, the two companies took 33% of the receipts for 28% of the mileage; the only real distortion was for Southend where they had 25% of the receipts for only 13% of the mileage. (There is, incidentally, no indication in the material surviving from 1852 to indicate why the lessees had been unable to negotiate more favourable tolls then, especially given that with Waddington's help they had been able to get the ECR working agreement arranged at rates that were scandalously favourable to them).

What was really exorbitant, however, was the situation that had applied since the opening of the Gas Factory Junction - Barking line in 1858, under which the ECR still took its full tolls (based on the Bow Junction - Forest Gate Junction mileage) for all the Fenchurch Street passenger traffic, which did not actually now run over ECR metals at all. The mileage actually run by LT&SR trains over the other companies' lines was now only two and three quarter miles, all on the L&BR, from Fenchurch Street to Gas Factory Junction; so that since 1858 the two companies were getting 33% of the fares to Tilbury for only 12% of the mileage, and 25% to Southend, for only 6% of the mileage. The Committee estimated that the 'excess' payments to the GER for mileage no longer actually run over at all were costing the LT&SR £6,822 pa, or, putting it another way, cutting the LT&SR's net profits to about 70% of what they would be otherwise. (This did not of course affect the shareholders who still got their 6%; and Peto Brassey & Betts could hardly complain too much about it given that they had agreed these tolls themselves in 1855/6 as a sop to evade ECR opposition when Peto wanted the 'Barking branch' built as a piece of anti-ECR politicking!). In fact, these tolls under the 1856 Act had been in dispute ever since 1858, and were currently under arbitration before John Hawkshaw who had been named in the Act for this purpose; an 'award' was in due course made in 1865.

The Committee also had much to say as to the inability of the shareholders to control the Board, as they only appointed 3 of the 9 Directors, the other 6 being primarily concerned with protecting the interests of the GER and L&BR. Indeed the GER and L&BR - appointed Directors were not even obliged to hold any LT&SR shares (and only one, Bishop, did hold any at this time).

The latter part of the report was taken up with an analysis of the line's present and future traffic. The Gravesend tripper traffic was noted to be 'diminishing yearly' now that there were so many rival resorts accessible elsewhere, and no hope was held out that it would ever return to former levels. However the town of Gravesend was still growing, so the residential traffic might continue to increase, although the SER's Charing Cross and Cannon Street extensions would make the SER route a greater rival. The Southend traffic should increase as the number of excursionists and 'families resident for the season' increased (in fact of course Southend was to attract all-year residents, rather than seasonal residents, for the most part). Steamboat competition would continue but 'you own the pier and you can therefore charge what dues you wish to the boats'. (This was not true; the LT&SR never owned Southend Pier at all, although Peto Brassey & Betts did rent it at this period). The local traffic at the stations between Bromley and Barking should increase as housing development occurred; indeed, 'a very large quantity of land between Plaistow and East Ham is (already) portioned off for building purposes'. The number of passengers off the NLR had fallen off latterly due to worsening connections but could be increased again by a new connection from Bow NLR to Bromley (for which see later). Such a connection, the Committee noted, would also enable the LT&SR to run its trains into Broad Street in future if the L&BR would not concede less exorbitant tolls. (The line to Broad Street was under construction by this date, and the L&BR were worried about its possible use by the LT&SR). On the goods front, the currently-meagre traffic could be boosted by the proposed docks at Dagenham (these, unfortunately, never came into being) and Tilbury (the 1860s Tilbury scheme never came off but the Committee were right in the long term).

The Committee said less than one might have expected on the matter of the excessively low fares charged (although they did suggest that the Gravesend fare could be increased by 2d). In fact the lessees had already put up the Gravesend fares in April 1858, and now did so again in March 1864:-

	1854	1859	1864
1st Single	1s 6d	1s 8d	2s 0d
1st Return	2s 6d	2s 9d	3s 0d
2nd Single	1s 0d	1s 2d	1s 4d
2nd Return	1s 8d	2s 0d	2s 4d

However, the whole of these increases were appropriated by the lessees to themselves, as 'ferry charges'! - this brought a dispute with the L&BR and ECR from 1859 on, as they considered that they should have a third of the extra. Other LT&S fares had not been increased.

(In 1865 Peto Brassey and Betts promoted an LT&SR Bill to have the maximum fares increased, seeking $1^1/_2$d per mile 1st class, 1d 2nd, and $^3/_4$d 3rd, instead of the existing 1d/ $^3/_4$d / $^1/_2$d. Seymour Clark the General Manager of the GNR, Forbes of the LC&DR and Alexander Sherriff the former General Manager of the NER, were brought before the parliamentary committee to testify that no railway could be made to pay at the present LT&SR fares. But, even though the lessees promised that the increased fares would only be applied to the one-fifth of LT&SR passengers travelling between two LT&SR stations, the Bill was thrown out by parliament).

After hearing the Investigatory Committee's report, the February 1864 shareholders' meeting elected Eley to the Board in place of Vardon. Lawrence and Cope were not due for re-election, but the meeting passed a resolution that 'Messrs Lawrence and Cope do not represent the interest of the shareholders, and sit on the Board against the wishes of the shareholders'. They would not be budged, however, and insisted on serving their time, Lawrence being replaced by Moxon in February 1865 and Cope going in February 1866.

Henceforth the L&BR and GER were obliged to take a less openly self-interested line on LT&SR affairs. In 1865 Daniell and Anderson both left the LT&SR Board for other reasons, and Eley was elected Chairman of the LT&SR (August 1865) and Moxon Deputy Chairman (February 1866). (Moxon died in 1869 and was replaced by George Stockdale).

THE END OF THE L&BR (1865)
The rivalry between the L&BR and the ECR had, as we have seen, been much exploited by Peto in the 1850s. However in the autumn of 1864 talks were conducted between the GER and the L&BR as to a proposed takeover of the L&BR by the GER; and a Bill was then promoted to this end in the 1865 session. The 'independent' LT&SR shareholders were far from pleased at this prospect, which would make them wholly dependent on the GER for access to London, and several leading shareholders asked Eley to convene a special Board meeting and move a resolution for opposing the Bill. The meeting was held on 16th February 1865 but Eley could not get the motion seconded, and it would of course have been defeated by the majority in any case. Eley then petitioned against the Bill on his own account, but withdrew for fear of the expense. Peto Brassey & Betts did petition, but to no avail. The Act was passed and the GER took over the L&BR on a 999-year lease as from 1.1.1866. The other 'foreign' companies running trains over the L&BR line had all obtained running powers as their price for not opposing the Bill, but the LT&SR, being unable to oppose the Bill as a result of the GER/L&BR majority on its Board, could not do so.

The L&BR company continued to exist, and with it the L&BR Directors on the LT&SR Board. But they were now to some extent puppets of the GER who effectively had 6/9 seats on the LT&SR Board from 1866.

ANOTHER LEASE TO THE GER PROPOSED (1865)
In March 1865, in the middle of the proceedings over the Bill for the L&BR takeover, the GER was approached by Peto Brassey & Betts with a new proposition for the GER to assume the lease of the LT&SR. The GER Board, annoyed at Peto Brassey & Betts' petitioning against their Bill, refused to discuss anything unless the petition was withdrawn. However, they asked Sinclair to report on the matter, and on 24th May he told the Traffic Committee that he would recommend the GER taking over the working of the LT&SR on the basis of taking all the receipts and charging the cost of working against them. The full GER Board approved this the next day, and asked the GER Solicitors to arrange an agreement with Peto Brassey & Betts. However, in July it was reported that they found the proposed terms (it is not clear exactly what was intended) objectionable. Nothing further is heard after this, save for the GER Board noting in November that 'no arrangements were contemplated'.

LOW STREET

Only one station, Low Street, was added to the LT&S system in the 1858-75 period (although this is not really a criticism of the lessees, as there were not any other locations calling for a station at this time).

In April 1861 the lessees were approached by the inhabitants of West Tilbury village to erect a station at Low Street level crossing. Such a station would also serve East Tilbury village, which was currently 3½ miles from a station (not that either village was of any great size). The station was approved by the Joint Committee on 7th May after Peto wrote that it 'will lead to a considerable amount of goods traffic being conveyed on the line, which now finds its way to London by water', and would serve 'the large Government forts now erecting at East Tilbury' (Coalhouse Fort). It was built quickly; the exact opening date is not known but it is in Bradshaw from July 1861.

The estimate was only £630 and this was reflected in the parsimonious facilities - 200ft platforms, a very plain brick building on the up platform, and a small goods shed and siding. There were no buildings at all on the down platform and no shelters. Very little changed subsequently (although additional sidings to serve a ballast pit were provided at the east end). The up platform was lengthened to 530ft in later LT&SR days, but the down platform remained at 200 ft until electrification. The two late 1950s views here show how the clock had stopped at 1861.

The upper view, looking down line on 19th September 1956 shows (left to right) the 1861

brick goods shed and sidings, the 8ft wide 'island' down platform, the 1861 main building (which comprised Gents/Ladies/Booking Hall/Booking Office) on the up side, the Midland signal box (which replaced the original 1881 box on the same site in 1925), and the 1854 Crossing Keeper's cottage. The bracketed signal was added in c1950, there having been no signal at that position previously. The signal box was odd in that its windows were not made to the standard sizes for Midland boxes. Under the new signalling of 1961 it was elevated on a new brick base (it is not at all evident why it had not been built of standard height in the first place).

The lower view is from the middle of the up platform in the misty winter sunshine of 23rd February 1958. Note the oil lighting which was eventually replaced by electric on electrification.

The crossing gates did not close fully across the line, as there were three tracks and the road was narrow. The goods shed (right) had a hipped roof but the front wall extended above eaves level.

Low Street was never a great success. The 'considerable goods traffic' never materialised and the station always vied with East Horndon for the honour of being the least remunerative on the LT&S. After East Tilbury Halt opened it became even less significant. The vicinity never attracted housing development and remains quite rural even today. The station closed on 5th June 1967 and only the privately occupied goods shed and the signal box remain in 1994.
(H. C. Casserley; Frank Church)

SOUTHEND 1872

The Southend of the 1872 OS Plan is still a small place, hardly expanded since the 1840s one inch map shown earlier save for one major development - Peto's 'Clifftown' of 1860. Not content with running the railway and pier, Peto also undertook this property development in order to start a residential traffic for the railway. In July 1859 he took a 99-year lease of 50 acres of land between the railway and the cliffs, still fields at this date. The August 1859 LT&S meeting was told 'he has given directions for the immediate erection of about fifty houses so as to be ready for occupation early in next year.....the directors believe that the accommodation which will be afforded for residence will materially improve the traffic of the railway'.

During 1860 a total of 124 houses were built in Clifftown Parade, Prittlewell Square, Runwell Terrace, Capel Terrace, Cashiobury Terrace, Devereux Terrace, Cambridge Terrace (now Cambridge Road), Nelson Terrace (now Nelson Street), and Scratton Road. It was christened

'Clifftown'. The road layout was such that all the houses had a sea view (or glimpse!) except for those in Scratton Road which overlooked the loco shed yard. The February 1861 meeting heard that all was completed.

Up to this date there had been no suitable trains to permit anyone living in Southend to travel to and from the city daily, but as from 1st March 1861 a Southend Express was put on, with 80-minute timings. The Illustrated London News of 1st June carried some publicity for the development, noting that 'arrangements have been entered into.....to issue season tickets at a reduced rate. The enterprise has been carried out with great spirit, and we trust it may be successful, as it helps to supply a want which the overworked middle classes of London experience'.

The houses found tenants but the development was not a big success. The development of 1860 covered only the eastern half of Peto's land. The western half was never proceeded with (although it will be seen here that some more ad hoc development had happened to the west by 1872).

Continued over

34

Middleton Brewery

Middleton Hotel

378ᵃ
2·452

401
·811

401
9·958

Crane

Terminus

399ᵃ
·151

B.M. 87·3

Railway Tavern

London Tavern

399
2·473

Milton Terrace

400
·378

400}
·136}

397
8·778

York Place

398
1·154

British School
(Boys & Girls)

SOU

Congregational
Chapel

Public Hall

Grove House

420
99·283

393
1·009

O   A   D

Post Office

Grave
Yard

Terrace

Royal Hotel

Pier Hotel

382
·928

ROYAL   TERRACE

B.M. 77·4

St. Jo

380
2·663

Baths

Seats

B.M. 28·6

High   Water   Mark   of

Ordinary   Tides

Wharf

Crane

HARBOUR

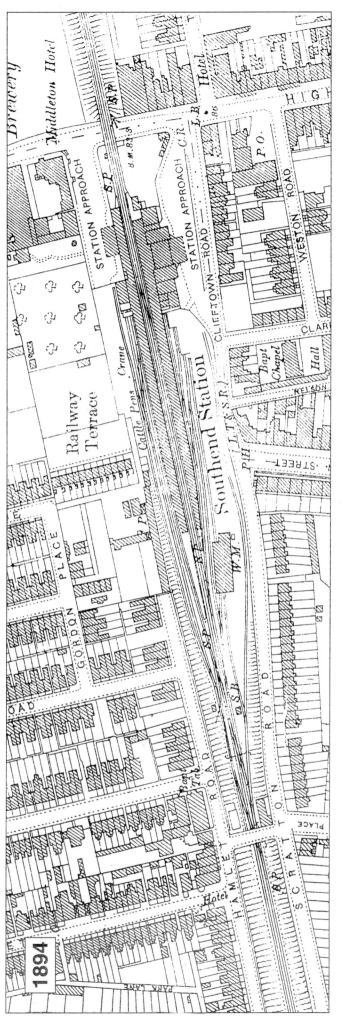

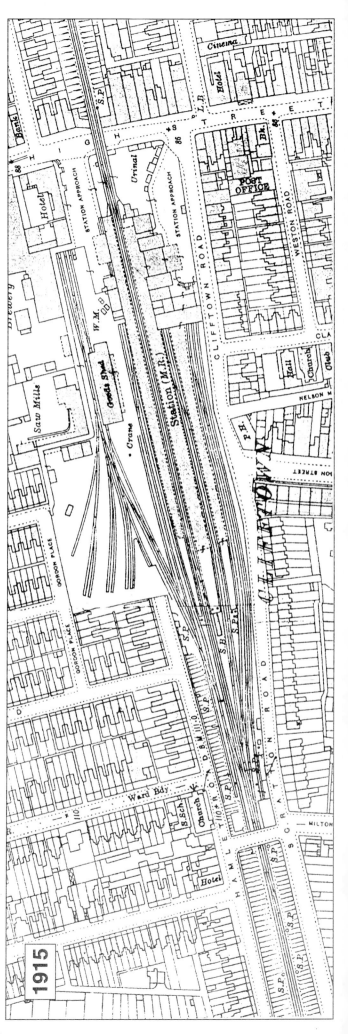

The 'Clifftown' estate was then split up in 1872 after Peto's bankruptcy. One of the factors retarding growth was Peto's urge to keep the place 'select', as a result of which the train timings were arranged to give only six and a half hours in the city, unsuitable for all but the most superior class of city man. This meant that few could live here and, therefore, that the trains could not be filled. Other developers of the period anxious to keep out the unsuitable also got caught by this difficulty elsewhere. The Southend residential traffic did not start to take off until the 1890s. The development of the Southend residential services from the 1870s on will be dealt with in Vol.2. Peto's 1860 new town remains largely intact today as a pleasant period piece, wholly unknown to the vast majority of visitors to Southend.

Southend station was still on the very edge of town in 1872, with undeveloped fields around it (although it will be seen that a small start has been made on property development north of the railway). The 1856 station (illustrated at Dow p.11) was much the most commodious of the original LT&S stations in passenger terms, with a 220ft long train shed, to which a goods shed was attached on the north side. The down side platform had been extended to the great length of 800ft in 1865, presumably for the reception of monster excursion trains. The up side platform was still only 400ft in 1872 although it was slightly extended soon after. On the south side was a two-road engine shed and loco yard with turntable. One is struck by the lack of siding capacity for putting away the stock of Bank Holiday excursions.

The next significant improvements of the station facilities came in 1881 when Scratton Road was diverted southwards at the east end (the new section, seen in the later OS extracts here, was named 'Clifftown Road'). The space so gained was initially used for goods sidings (but in 1889 became the new station forecourt). Also in 1881 the loco shed was extended - something of a wasted expenditure as the shed closed a few years later after Shoeburyness shed opened - and a large porte-cochere was erected against the end wall of the train shed, as seen in one of Dow's illustrations. This was for the convenience of visitors to the Essex Show, held at Southend in 1881, and it was removed in 1882 for

the extension of the line to Shoeburyness. This extension, opened in 1884, had comparatively little impact on the station as it simply went through the end wall.

The original signal hut is shown on this 1872 plan (by the 'S.P.'). It was replaced by an interlocked signal box in 1881 but was to survive for many years as a store hut, removed to the down side of the line (it can be seen in Dow's frontispiece view).

SOUTHEND 1894 *left*

The LT&SR spent many years considering the possibility of a new station at Southend, but it was postponed until the impending arrival of the GER in the town. The main contract was given to Lucas & Aird for £17,619 in November 1888, for completion by May 1889. The new buildings were on the site of the 1856 buildings which were wholly removed. They were of red brick, with large porte-cocheres on both the up and the down sides. Both platforms were widened and provided with lengthy canopies, and the up platform was extended westwards, so that there were now four platforms (up and down main, and a bay each side) capable of dealing with normal length trains. The main lines remained on the original alignment, and some of the connections at the west end remained as before; otherwise the track layout was all new in 1889, as the platform alterations required the rearrangement of the goods sidings on both sides.

This 1894 OS extract shows the 1889 Southend station. The signal box is that of 1881 which survived the 1889 changes. The replacement goods shed on the up side was built c1883.

SOUTHEND 1915 *left*

Although the station buildings of 1889 have survived to the present day, there was a massive expansion of the layout, to the form shown on this 1915 OS extract, in 1899. This was prompted by the need for extra platform accommodation for the summer traffic, and by the inadequacy of the goods accommodation as the town's popula-

tion increased. The work was approved by the LT&SR Board in November/December 1898, and a contract given to Mowlem. Basically a new island platform (5 and 6) was built on the up side, with two carriage sidings to the south of it, on the site of the former up side goods sidings. The existing up platform (3 and 4) was widened to accommodate better the returning summer evening crowds; the widening of the canopy on this platform, with a third line of columns, is still detectable today. The goods facilities were wholly transferred to the down side with new sidings and a new (the third) goods shed on newly acquired land. The houses of 'Railway Terrace' were removed for this. Apart from the main lines and the north side bay (Platform 1) all the track layout was once again wholly new. A new signal box was provided at the west end of Platforms 3/4. The works were inspected by Col Addison in September 1899 although not fully completed at that date.

After 1899 there was little change until electrification, the only work of note being the enlargement of the goods shed in 1929. In the late 1950s the platforms were all extended at the west end, and the connections all altered in consequence. A new panel signal box opened in October 1960 but otherwise there was no major change until the rationalisations of the 1970s and 1980s when the goods yard was closed and lifted and Platforms 5 and 6, unwanted since the collapse of the day-tripper traffic, were removed. Now only Platforms 1-4 remain and the canopies have been cut back.

The track layout at the west end is poorly drawn by the OS; there were always direct connections from the down main into Platforms 4-6.

below

Southend station's 1900s-1950s heyday is epitomised in this fine view of No.59 Holloway awaiting departure in Platform 6 with one of the regular St.Pancras trains, c1910. The 1899 canopy on this platform was built in the same style as the 1889 canopies on the other platforms.
(R.C.Riley collection).

Bradshaw Timetable for February 1863. Note the Barking 'shorts' at 10.20, 11.50, 2.5, 3.22, 5.22 and 7.37 down, and 9.0, 11.10, 1.20, 2.40, 4.10 and 6.20 up. These had been introduced in 1858, no doubt with hopes of fostering a suburban traffic, but in fact they had only increased to eight each way by 1875. The down ones also seem to be timed to 'relieve' the main down trains.

Connections from the NLR via Stepney are shown. Note that the fares from all NLR stations to LT&S stations were the same as the fares from Fenchurch Street, so passengers from the western end of the NLR line got an even better bargain than most!

The four-trains-a-day service from Bishopsgate is still shown as 'Eastern Counties', Bradshaw having forgotten to change it to 'Great Eastern'.

Gravesend Terrace Pier still appears in the timetable setting, four years after the LT&S boats had ceased calling there. The note about boats not running to Rosherville Pier in foggy weather always appeared in the timetables.

Note the Southend 'expresses' at 8.20am up and 4.25pm down, introduced in 1861. A full account of the 'expresses' is given in Chapter 9.

For comparison, the previous summer's timetable differed only in having an additional 8.22am to Southend (the 7.50am running only to Tilbury); the 9.7pm down extended to Southend; the 7.40am up starting from Southend; one extra Barking 'short' each way; and an enhanced service on Sundays.

Any attempt to work out the trainset workings for the timetables of this period inevitably results in a conclusion that there would have been various possible ways of arranging it! However one can see that the timetable here involves six trainsets; two based at Southend, two at the London end, one at Tilbury, and one at Barking which works all the 'shorts'.

LONDON, TILBURY, and SOUTHEND.

[Bradshaw timetable for February 1863 — dense tabular matter reproduced in the image, with "Down." "Week Days." and "Sundays." sections listing stations including Fenchurch St., Stepney, Chalk Farm, Camden Road, Caledonian Rd, Islington, Newington Road, Kingsland, Hackney, Victoria Park, Bow, Bromley, Plaistow, East Ham, Barking, Bishopsgate, Mile End, Stratford, Forest Gate, Rainham, Purfleet, Grays, Tilbury, Low Street, Stanford-le-Hope, Pitsea, Benfleet, Leigh, Southend, Gravesend.]

FARES — From any Station on the North London Line to:

	ORDINARY.		RETURN TICKETS.	
	1st class	2nd class	1st class	2nd class
	s. d.	s. d.	s. d.	s. d.
Plaistow	0 6	0 4	0 9	0 6
East Ham	0 9	0 6	1 0	0 9
Barking	1 0	0 9	1 8	1 3
Rainham, Purfleet, or Grays	1 6	1 0	..	..
Tilbury or Gravesend	1 8	1 2	2 9	2 0
Low Street or Stanford-le-Hope	2 0	1 6	..	..
Pitsea	3 0	2 4	..	..
Benfleet or Leigh	3 6	2 ..	..	..
Southend	3 8	2 6	5 10	4 2

a Go to Rosherville. ☞ The Boats do not go to Rosherville in foggy weather.

FARES.—London to Gravesend, 1st class, 1s. 8d.; 2nd, 1s. 2d.: to Southend, 3s. 6d.; 2s. 6d. RETURN TICKETS.—London to Gravesend, 2s. 9d.; 2s: to Southend, 5s. 10d.: 4s. 2d.: those issued on Saturday are available until Monday.

A. Wightman.

STAGNATION (1866-75)

After 1866 Peto Brassey & Betts ceased to be a real force in the politics of the LT&SR. Their representatives on the Board had gone, replaced by genuine shareholders' representatives. Then in May 1866 Peto & Betts were bankrupted; and when Brassey's death followed in 1870, the lease was left in the hands of Brassey's executors, whose interest was a purely legal one with a minimal active involvement. The railway was run by their 'Manager' Joseph Louth (who had taken that post, after some years as Assistant Manager, on Wightman's death in the autumn of 1864). The fact that the lease had only five years to run no doubt contributed to the de facto decision to let things drift until the end.

The shareholders' Directors considered that insufficient attempt was being made to attract traffic; Eley stated in 1870 that 'he was dissatisfied with the management of the line. He thought that the lessees might develop the traffic, but they had declined to go to any expense for so doing in consequence of the excessive tolls they had to pay'. But one suspects that, with the London suburban area still in the earliest stages of development, and the Southend residential traffic similarly, there was not a lot of extra traffic available immediately, even if an effort had been made.

Very little capital expenditure was undertaken on the line after 1858, and no extra capital had to be authorised after the 1856 Act until 1875.

PASSENGER TRAIN SERVICES 1858-1875

The diversion of all LT&S trains to the Gas Factory Junction-Barking line in March 1858 saw a 7-minute reduction of journey times for those trains which now ran fast from Stepney to Barking, but only 2 minutes for those which called at all stations. However punctuality must have been much improved.

In the early 1860s the number of trains running on from Tilbury to Southend was increased to six or seven (from the 3-5 of the first years), the services on the London-Tilbury leg remaining at ten or eleven as before. After this the whole LT&SR timetable quite stagnated until after the end of the lease (although one must again say that it was not a particularly bad timetable for the time, and the area served: the Board minutes do not mention any 'memorials' being received for better services).

THE WORKING OF THE LINE UNDER THE LESSEES

Very little survives as to the details of the operation of the LT&S line in the lessees' period.

The railway was run by Wightman, and then by his successor Louth, as Manager to the lessees. Both of them also held the post of Superintendent of the L&BR line (after 1865 Louth was of course a GER employee in this capacity rather than an L&BR employee), and they ran the LT&S line from their 'L&B' offices at Fenchurch Street. As the LT&SR Company Secretary Kennell was also Secretary to the L&BR, and likewise did the LT&S work from his L&BR office, the LT&SR accordingly did not have any separate office of its own at all, and indeed was physically inseparable from the L&BR in terms of its senior officers!

Under the Manager were the other Peto Brassey & Betts employees, i.e. station staff and line maintenance staff. There were few signalmen as the line was run on the 'time interval' system with the station staff working the signals. Indeed when Stride took over as Manager in 1875 at the end of the lease, he discovered there was no Rule Book either! - and things seem to have been fairly relaxed in general. The 'Engineering

Department' (not that such a term was used) was really only the regular line maintenance gangs, for the new works undertaken after 1858 were mostly only minor track alterations, platform reconstructions, etc that were within their capabilities. A Smithy and a Joiner's Shop existed at Tilbury by 1865.

Bidder and Fowler remained in theory the LT&SR Engineers, but in practice they did nothing after 1858 beyond producing special reports on the state of the line at the Board's request in 1859 and 1865 (after which they are not heard of again, although they were still named as the company's Engineers in Bradshaw's Manual in the 1870s). In June 1868 the GER Engineers produced a report on the LT&S line at the request of the GER Locomotive Committee who were concerned for their locomotives' running; Louth accompanied them on an inspection trip and promised afterwards to commence the renewal of the 1854 permanent way which was still in situ (mostly unfishplated) at this date. Further evidence that Bidder was effectively out of it comes in August 1869 when the LT&SR Board asked Eley to confer with Brassey about starting a 6-monthly inspection of the line by 'an Engineer to be selected by the Board' (there is no evidence that this actually happened).

As to the working of the trains by the ECR/GER, there were locomotive sheds on the line at Tilbury and Southend, but much of the work was done by Stratford locos. The locos used for working the LT&S were not a separate stock kept for LT&S purposes, but part of the ordinary ECR fleet; those based at Tilbury and Southend at any particular time were naturally given over to LT&S line work, but Stratford would use different locos

on different days for their LT&S line duties. The timetabled LT&S services only required 8-10 locos, but excursions, 'boat trains', cattle specials etc could mean up to 15 needed on some days. The sixteen Gooch 2-2-2Ts built for the opening of the LT&S in 1853-5 continued to see much use on the line, but other types also saw regular use on the LT&S, notably the Sinclair 'Y' Class 2-4-0s, and in later years the Johnson 'Little Sharpie' 2-4-0s, the Johnson '477' Class 0-6-0s (for goods work), and the Johnson '134' Class 0-4-4Ts. In the lessees' period locomotives normally worked through from Fenchurch Street to Southend (unlike later), backing their trains into Tilbury station from East Junction to avoid having to run round (and from West Jn on the up journey).

Coaching stock was also kept at Tilbury and Southend, where (almost) all trains terminated. There was a Carriage Shed at Tilbury (but this was burned down in 1878). The LT&S line carriages were kept separate; the number required for the daily scheduled services never rose above the original 60 or so. However additional carriages were brought in from the general ECR fleet on busy days in the summer. An ECR minute notes that 157 coaches were in use on LT&S services on one day in July 1860.

NLR CONNECTIONS AND THE BOW-BROMLEY BRANCH

The populous suburbs served by the North London Railway were seen as a source of a potentially large traffic to Gravesend and Southend in particular, but in practice it had not always

The LT&S line was hardly photographed prior to the late 1890s, and not a single photograph has ever come to light of an LT&S train in the days of the lessees. Similarly the loco shed at Southend is unrecorded. However this one photograph survives of the original timber Tilbury loco shed, which was replaced by the new shed in 1906.

The photographer is standing on the South Jn - West Jn curve looking northwest, some time in the 1890s, but with some of the atmosphere of earlier days still surviving. The locomotive facilities comprised only the two shed roads themselves, plus the two short sidings in the foreground used (as here) for coal wagons and locomotives being coaled. And this was the most important LT&S shed up to this period! So far as can be proved from limited sources, the shed building did date from 1854.

To the left of the running lines are the two (note the points at left edge) carriage sidings. The carriage stock at far left here is however on the 1886 through line to Tilbury Docks Tidal Basin.

In the background is one of the three rows of 'Railway Cottages'.

Note the use of full-size signals to control the exit from the loco sidings, and the absence of trap points.

The water supply at Tilbury proved terribly salty. In 1861 a well was dug at Low Street (at the same time as the station was being built) and Tilbury shed had its water piped from this well subsequently, into BR days.

(A. G. Ellis collection)

proved possible to arrange good connections. The changing patterns of services had seen many alterations on this front; so far as daily scheduled services were concerned, the fate of passengers wishing to change from the NLR to the LT&S line had been as follows:-

April 1854 - Passengers changed at Stepney, from the NLR trains into Fenchurch Street, into the Fenchurch Street portions of LT&S trains. With the NLR trains running every 1/4 hour, this was reasonably convenient, albeit involving an element of 'backtracking' to Gas Factory Jn which no doubt irritated some!

October 1854 - With the opening of the Victoria Park-Stratford line, very good connections were now provided to LT&S trains at Stratford, passengers travelling in through Hampstead Road-Stratford coaches which were detached from the main NLR train at Victoria Park.

March 1858 - The opening of the Gas Factory Jn-Barking line put a stop to connections at Stratford, and the original changing at Stepney was resumed. This brought a falling off of traffic.

November 1865 - The opening of the Broad Street line meant that NLR passengers from west of Dalston Junction now had to change there as well (albeit that connections there were very quick).

August 1866 - The replacement of the Broad Street-Fenchurch Street service by a Broad Street-Poplar service plus a Bow-Fenchurch Street shuttle, both 1/4-hourly still, meant that all NLR passengers now had to change at both Bow and Stepney to reach the LT&S trains (plus a third change at Dalston Junction for those from west of there).

September 1866 - The new situation being admitted as unsatisfactory, a very convenient Chalk Farm-Victoria Park-Stratford-Barking through service was introduced by the NLR with the GER's agreement, eleven trains a day giving connections into all LT&SR trains at Barking. Unfortunately this had to be abandoned after nine weeks as it caused too many operating problems in the congestion at Stratford. (One of the NLR trains actually collided with a GER goods at Stratford on 10th September, injuring 20 passengers).

November 1866 - Reversion to the August 1866 situation. As a result the number of passengers fell off again.

In addition, through trains had been run daily by the NLR to Tilbury (via Hackney Wick-Stratford) in the summer of 1855, and through excursions to Southend (by the same route) at various times.

As mentioned earlier, the LT&SR shareholders' committee in 1864 recommended a direct NLR-LT&SR link at Bow, both to improve regular connections and with the 'political' aim of being able to run LT&SR trains into Broad Street instead of Fenchurch Street. On the goods front, the (limited) traffic between the LT&SR and the 'northern lines' was currently exchanged at Stratford - the LT&SR goods trains still ran via Stratford, and not via Plaistow, to enable this - but in 1866 the cattle specials from Thames Haven to Maiden Lane began, and with great hopes being held for this traffic, it was another reason to seek a direct link to the NLR. However, the LT&SR could not really promote such a link itself, since the GER majority on its Board would not be likely to countenance it, the existing situation whereby the LT&SR was entirely dependent on GER metals for access to the outside world being much more to

their liking!

It was therefore necessary for the NLR to take up the idea if it were to get anywhere. The NLR saw no reason to favour the LT&SR over the GER, but they did want improved connections from their line to the east. They held talks with the GER in 1866 but these did not produce results, not from cantankerousness on either side but simply on account of the old problem of the congested state of the GER line. Accordingly the NLR was driven to favour an LT&SR link, and deposited plans for a Bow-Bromley curve in November 1866, after which they (and the LNWR) began negotiations with the LT&SR and the lessees for the NLR and LNWR to be given running powers over the LT&S system. The 'independent' LT&SR directors were keen to have such powers granted, and by dint of two of the L&BR directors voting with them (for reasons not explained) and the exercise of the Chairman's casting vote, they were actually able to get the proposed running powers agreement approved by the LT&SR board in March 1867. The agreement was dated 20th March 1867 (and was later confirmed by the LNWR (Additional Powers) Act 1871).

The NLR Bill was initially opposed by the GER, but this was dropped and the Act was passed, without opposition to the curve in committee, on 17th June 1867. After some delays over land, the contract was let to Waring Bros in March 1868. To avoid having to demolish Bow Works, it was necessary for the line to begin at the north end of Bow station, as a result of which the station had to be rebuilt with four platforms. The line rose to come alongside the LT&S line at Devons Road, but was continued parallel to it, with the junction made at St Leonards Street. The interlocked signal box here at 'Bromley Junction' was the first on the LT&S (although it was actually built by the NLR, who would have had to pay for it in any case). The double-track line was 51ch long in its original form. After inspection by Tyler it opened for excursions on 17th May 1869 and for the regular passenger service on the 18th. (When the new Bromley station was built west of St Leonards Street in 1893, the NLR junction was moved further west - see the maps in Chapter 8).

At this period the LNWR had grand ideas in the back of its mind as to the benefits that might accrue from the LT&S connection. These ideas manifested themselves in 1870 when a large area of land at Thames Haven was purchased by the LNWR from Brassey (who had acquired it some years previously for speculative purposes), clearly in the hope of building dock facilities there to give the LNWR better access to Thames shipping. (This LNWR Thames Haven scheme never materialised, and the land was sold off in 1902). Then in 1871 the LNWR promoted a branch from the LT&SR at Upper Abbey Mills Junction to the Victoria Dock north side sidings; but this was abandoned in Parliament. In 1873/4 the possibility of the LNWR taking over the LT&SR was aired (see below) but again came to nothing.

Most grandiose of all was the possibility of the Bow-Bromley curve being used for Continental boat trains from Manchester to Dover. This arose in 1876 when the LNWR took a definite interest in the proposed 'London Essex & Kent Coast Junction Railway', which involved a tunnel under the Thames from the LT&SR west of Purfleet, giving connections to the SER at Stone, the LC&DR at Farningham Road, and the LC&DR at Eynsford. This was a speculative scheme by origin, evolved by the engineers Benjamin Haughton and William Lawford in combination with financiers; but Haughton and Lawford had good LNWR contacts, having both held senior posts with the LNWR before setting up in private practice, and they persuaded William Cawkwell, the LNWR Director (and former Manager), to support the scheme in parliament with such enthusiasm that it became seen as an LNWR-backed plot. The LT&SR were in favour (although a back seat was taken); the SER and LC&DR against as they would lose mileage on traffic for Kent currently exchanged in central London. The LE&KCJR did get its Act, but once again the LNWR failed to translate moral support into financial support, and the scheme soon faded away. (This was the first of several Thames Tunnel schemes involving lines from the LT&SR in the Purfleet/Grays area. There was a rival 'North & South (Gravesend Tunnel) Junction Railway' in 1876; a

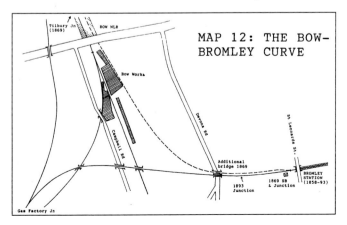

MAP 12: THE BOW-BROMLEY CURVE

'Tilbury & Gravesend Tunnel Junction Railway' in 1882; a 'Purfleet & Gravesend Junction Railway' in 1900; and a 'Lower Thames Tunnel Railways' in 1907. The LT&SR was not actually involved in any of them, and none of them ever came anywhere near getting off the ground).

The LNWR's great ideas of what might be achieved from the Bromley connection were, therefore, all destined to non-fulfilment. The only facility which the LNWR actually ever provided off the LT&S system was a ballast siding at Upton Park in 1874 which, after being removed in the '80s, was reopened in 1895 as an LNWR public Goods & Coal Depot. The goods trains to Upton Park were run by the NLR on the LNWR's behalf, and the LNWR themselves never exercised their running powers over the LT&SR at all. However, occasional military and other specials were run through to LT&S destinations with LNWR locos in later decades, by agreement.

The passenger services run by the NLR over the curve are dealt with in the insert here. It was not much used for goods traffic until 1876 when the main LT&SR goods trains were eventually diverted via Plaistow instead of Stratford and began exchanging traffic for the 'northern lines' at Plaistow; the Thames Haven cattle trains also ran this way from 1876. The LT&SR never found it necessary to seek to run its own trains into Broad Street, although this was to be done for some LT&S line trains from 1923 to 1935 when Fenchurch Street became overcrowded.

PASSENGER TRAIN SERVICES BETWEEN THE NLR AND THE LT&SR AFTER 1869

DAILY SERVICES

From 18th May 1869 a daily NLR Chalk Farm-Plaistow service was introduced, eight trains each way connecting with most (but not all) LT&S services at Plaistow. Plaistow was probably chosen as the terminus (which it remained until the service's end) because more LT&SR trains stopped there than at Bromley, and because it had a siding which could be used for the train's layover, whereas Bromley had no sidings at all at this date. This service was no doubt regarded by its users as a great improvement on the previous situation, but sadly it proved unremunerative.

From 1st October 1871, therefore, it was replaced by a Bow-Plaistow shuttle, still run by the NLR, bringing back the need for two or three changes. This consisted of ten journeys each way giving connections into all LT&SR trains going beyond Barking.

From 1st June 1877 the Chalk Farm-Plaistow service resumed, after discussions between the LT&SR and NLR since 1875, the new LT&SR management wishing to see better connections. But it once again proved unviable.

So from 1st February 1878 the Bow-Plaistow shuttle resumed again, this time destined to stay. It began at the previous 10 trains each way, but as the LT&S line services increased it was stepped up correspondingly, reaching 23 each way by 1885. With a journey time of only six minutes, this could still be worked by one trainset, although there were some tight turnarounds of as little as four minutes at Plaistow. A bay platform was provided at Plaistow for the NLR trains (on the north side) in 1880; they used this until 1905 when they transferred to the new bay platform No 6 on the south side, using the 'Through' lines between Bromley and Plaistow. At Bow a runround siding was provided for the Plaistow shuttle to the north of the station. The shuttle was itself not very profitable, an NLR study in 1905 showing annual receipts of £151 against an annual running cost of £1,059, although this excluded the 'contributory revenue' it generated. The number of trips was reduced in the 1900s and was down to 13 each way by 1913. The service finally ceased as from 1st January 1916.

Through tickets between NLR and LT&S line stations were still issued after 1916, the passengers being obliged to walk between Bow NLR and Bow Road (District), until 1945. Parcels traffic after 1916 went to St Pancras and was carted to Euston.

'MARGATE' THROUGH COACHES (1869-86)

In the summers of 1869-75 and 1877-80, through coaches were run from Chalk Farm daily (as extra trains on the NLR section) for attaching at Plaistow to the LT&SR Fenchurch Street-Thames Haven (for Margate) Boat Trains. The timings in 1880 were:

10.10am from Chalk Farm, daily
2.47pm from Gospel Oak, Saturdays

6.50pm from Thames Haven, daily (arr Chalk Farm 8.15pm)
12.5pm from Thames Haven, Mondays (arr Chalk Farm 1.27pm)
There was no LT&SR 'Margate' service at all in the summers of 1876 and 1881, hence the NLR coaches did not run in those years. However in the summer of 1882 the service resumed, but to Tilbury instead of Thames Haven. In 1882-5 the NLR coaches were attached at Plaistow as before, and can be seen in the 1883 timetable in Chapter 6. But when the LT&SR introduced the Westinghouse brake in 1885/6 instead of the Clarke & Webb chain brake which both companies had been using, it became difficult to run combined trains, so in 1886 the NLR ran a complete train through to Tilbury; this unfortunately affected the profitability.

SOUTHEND THROUGH SERVICES (1869-86)

In the summers of 1869 to 1886, the NLR also ran complete through trains, on Sundays and Mondays only, from Chalk Farm to Southend (one train down in the morning and back in the evening). These called at all stations to Bow (also at Plaistow latterly) and then ran non-stop to Tilbury (for Gravesend and steamboat trippers) and Southend. The 1883 timetable in Chapter 6 shows typical timings. One assumes that an LT&SR Pilotman was provided for the NLR drivers east of Plaistow.

After the 1886 season the NLR withdrew the 'Margate' and Southend timetabled services. The NLR minutes do not record the reason, but figures quoted in autumn 1886 show limited profits, and the LT&SR Chairman stated in 1888 that the NLR had given up because of the poor economics. Subsequent writers have instead put the withdrawal down to the fact that, thanks to the different braking systems, LT&SR locos would no longer be able to 'rescue' any NLR train that failed in darkest Essex, but this would really only have applied after 1891 when the NLR changed to the vacuum brake. LT&S locos could have hauled a chainbraked NLR train in an emergency in the 1886-91 period. And in any case the LT&SR were quite happy to let the Midland run through to Southend after 1894; their trains were similarly 'unrescueable' then.

In addition to the above booked services, it seems that excursions were still run by the NLR to Southend on Bank Holidays after 1869 - for example, it was stated at the LT&SR August 1871 meeting that there had been 'a big traffic from the NLR' on that August Holiday Monday, the implication being that this was in extra trains.

It has been implied elsewhere that no through excursion trains, either, were run by the NLR to Southend in the summers of 1887 to 1906, but this does not appear to be correct; if there was a 'gap' it was a brief one. An article in The Locomotive Magazine implies that excursions had run throughout, and there are other clear references to NLR excursions to Southend having run in 1898 at least. The article refers to the LT&SR's decision to fit four locos with the vacuum brake in 1897 as having been motivated by NLR excursions (inter alia), and it seems that thereafter any NLR excursions were hauled east of Plaistow by these LT&S locos, rather than the NLR loco running through.

LT&SR THROUGH SERVICES (1907-1914)

As the daytripper traffic on ordinary summer weekdays increased, the idea of running timetabled through trains was aired again, and came to pass in the summer of 1907, with a daily through train from Chalk Farm to Southend and back, run from 1.6.07 to 31.10.07. This service comprised an LT&SR loco and train (with an NLR Pilotman west of Plaistow). The coaches carried destination boards reading 'CHALK FARM - SOUTHEND THROUGH TRAIN 2/6 RETURN DAILY'. The trains naturally now ran via the Upminster line, fast between Bow and Leigh, enabling a journey time of only 1hr 33 mins from Chalk Farm to Southend.

The service was deemed a success, despite 1907 being a poor summer, and was repeated in the years following. From 1910 there were two trains on Sundays. The timings of the service in the summer 1913 WTT were:-

WEEKDAYS
8.22am ECS Plaistow - Chalk Farm 9.14am
9.18am Chalk Farm - Southend 10.51am
7.32pm Southend - Chalk Farm 9.2pm
9.7pm ECS Chalk Farm - Plaistow 9.42pm
SUNDAYS
(1)
7.4am ECS Plaistow - Chalk Farm 7.36am
7.52am ECS Chalk Farm, 7.56am Camden Road - Southend 9.24am
6.48pm Southend - Camden Road 8.12pm
thence ECS to Chalk Farm 8.15pm
8.24pm ECS Chalk Farm - Tilbury
(2)
9.10am ECS Plaistow - Chalk Farm 9.50am
10.5am ECS Chalk Farm, 10.8am Camden Road - Southend 11.32am
8.36pm Southend - Camden Road 10.12pm
thence ECS to Chalk Farm 10.15pm
10.24pm ECS Chalk Farm - Barking

On the busiest days a relief train was run, consisting of an NLR loco and train through to Southend (with LT&SR Pilotman from Plaistow). The NLR loco was serviced at Shoeburyness during the day. The NLR had no running powers via Upminster but could of course run by agreement. There were however no through trains now on Bank Holidays, as there were no paths available.

The services ended at the outbreak of the First World War. H.V. Borley concluded that the last date on which the trains actually ran was 31st July 1914.

After 1914 there were never again any timetabled through services. But excursions from the NLR and L&NWR lines continued to run regularly to Southend via Bow and Bromley until the curve was closed to all traffic in 1959.

On August Bank Holiday Tuesday, 5th August 1913, it was necessary to run the NLR relief train to Southend. It is seen here at Cranham, photographed by Ken Nunn.
(Ken Nunn LCGB)

THE REVOLUTION THAT FAILED: THE LT&SR 1874 BILL

As the end of the lease approached, the LT&SR - that is to say, Eley and the other 'independent' directors - were in a difficult position. They had no means of running the line themselves after July 1875, and anything they sought to do might be prevented by the GER majority on the Board. Eley tried from 1872 to negotiate with the GER as to the future running of the line, but they merely rejected all his suggestions without making any constructive proposition themselves.

The 'independent' directors therefore concluded that they must make a move to have the GER and L&BR directors on the LT&SR Board removed, and establish the company on a normal footing. The August 1873 shareholders' meeting approved an application to parliament to this end, and a Bill was promoted in 1874. Eley told the House of Commons committee in May 1874 that the present situation was intolerable, with continual conflict between the majority of the Board and the three shareholders' representatives, and no independent staff at the latter's disposal. 'I have been taunted by the Great Eastern Directors that we are powerless and they they have powers over us and we have none over them', he complained.

The 1874 Bill also sought running powers over the GER to Fenchurch Street and Liverpool Street. No such running powers had been granted in 1862 when the LT&SR was made a separate company, and as things stood the LT&SR would have no rights at all after the end of the lease.

However the Bill was rejected by the Commons Committee on 7th May 1874. Eley and Stockdale than resigned from the Board in August, partly because they were not in good health and partly because it was felt by Eley that he had made himself persona non grata with the GER. A private meeting was held of LT&SR shareholders holding over £1,000 stock to choose successors, and they decided upon Charles Bischoff* and Henry Doughty Browne,** who held no less than £150,000 stock. At a special shareholders' meeting on 15th September, Bischoff was elected Chairman and Doughty Browne Deputy Chairman.

Shortly afterwards, the GER Chairman Lightly Simpson resigned on 4th November 1874, being replaced by Charles Henry Parkes.

During 1873/4 Eley had talks with the GNR, NLR, and LNWR as to possible involvements by those companies in the working of the LT&SR after July 1875, but these did not produce any definite results. In October 1874 the GER and LNWR also discussed the subject of the LT&SR's future, but the GER were assured that neither the LNWR nor the NLR had any desire to lease or work the LT&SR.

* *Charles Bischoff (1801-1896), stockbroker, not involved with any other railway company. Retired as LT&SR Chairman January 1883 on age grounds, but remained on the Board until 1893!*

**Henry Doughty Browne (1837-1907). Stockbroker. Joined the Stock Exchange 1858 and later became a leading figure in its administration, as a 'Trustee and Manager'. When appointed to the LT&SR Board and chosen as Deputy Chairman in 1874, he had already had a little dabbling in railways; he is listed as a Director of the Northern Railway of Buenos Aires in 1873, and then became involved with Alexander Young's 'Imperial Credit Co. Ltd.' syndicate which controlled several small British companies. In the 1880s he was a Director of the Grand Trunk Railway of Canada, where he had Lord Claud Hamilton as a colleague. In his last years he was Chairman of the Alabama New Orleans Texas & Pacific Junction Railways, and of the Anglo-Argentine Tramways Co. None of these diverse interests really impinged on the LT&SR 'politically', however. Via the LT&SR he became a Director of the T&FG and the W&B.*

Chairman of the LT&SR from January 1883, when Bischoff vacated the chair owing to his age, Doughty Browne's position naturally made him a very important figure in the company's affairs in the 1880s and 1890s. He was taken seriously ill in 1904 and resigned the chair for health reasons in January 1906, but remained on the Board until his death on 2nd January 1907. The Railway News noted

'By the City at large he was held in the highest esteem, as embodying all that was best in what is often affectionally termed 'the Old School'.'

CHAPTER 4

Taking Control (1875-1881)

THE GER AGREEMENT (1875-6)

Bischoff and Doughty Browne, the LT&SR's new Chairman and Deputy Chairman, immediately set about a resumption of the previous efforts at negotiating with the GER over the future of the line. However in October 1874 a formal statement was received from the GER Chairman Lightly Simpson that the GER 'would not be prepared to make any proposition with regard to the future working of the line.'

Bischoff had no previous railway experience himself and, having no independent senior 'LT&SR' officers to assist him, he decided that he must seek outside professional assistance on the policy to be pursued. His choice fell on Underdown the General Manager of the Manchester Sheffield & Lincolnshire Railway. At the same time a parliamentary application was prepared for the 1875 session, seeking (inter alia) powers to make a working agreement with, lease the line to, or sell the company to, any of the GER, NLR, LNWR, Midland, or GNR. (These clauses were later withdrawn from the Bill in parliament, when arrangements were sorted out with the GER).

After C.H. Parkes became GER Chairman in November, the negotiations with the GER soon took a much more positive form. Parkes was himself a substantial LT&SR shareholder of many years' standing, and had taken an active interest, in that capacity, since the 1862/3 controversies; he had also been appointed to the LT&SR Board latterly, albeit as a GER representative. Furthermore, he also quickly established a good personal relationship with Bischoff, which was to be of great value to the LT&SR in the years that followed. On 5th November 1874 (the day after Parkes assumed the Chair) there was a meeting at Bishopsgate between the GER Board and the LT&SR Directors at which the former, whilst reiterating that they were not willing to lease the LT&S line, conceded that they would 'work it for a time ... in the circumstances' to resolve the immediate problem of how the trains would be run after July 1875, although they would prefer that the LT&SR should start working their line directly as soon as possible.

Underdown made an inspection of the line, as a result of which it was decided in January 1875 to appoint William Lawford as Engineer to the LT&SR company 'to report on the present condition of the line prior to the expiry of the lease'. (Lawford's name has already been mentioned in Chapter 3 in the context of his private involvement, a few months after this, in the promotion of the 'London Essex & Kent Coast Junction Railway'). Lawford made a report on 31st March.

Underdown also had discussions with the GER General Manager, Swarbrick, as to the future working of the line. All hope of a long-term arrangement was abandoned by February 1875 when the LT&SR Board informed the shareholders that they 'saw no prospect of a lease being agreed'. Why the GER would not consider any long-term lease or working agreement at this time, when the LT&SR were coming to them as active suitors, is not fully explained. The GER in later years were of course to come to rue the attitude taken in 1874/5, for it meant that the GER threw away an open chance to make the LT&S line part of their own system in the same way as they had taken control of the L&BR ten years previously.

Negotiations on a temporary working arrangement, however, and on the permanent future arrangements for running powers and tolls for LT&S trains into Fenchurch Street, proceeded to a satisfactory end quite quickly. A draft agreement was produced on 23rd March 1875, and was approved by the LT&SR Board on 4th May and by a special LT&SR shareholders' meeting on 25th May. Thus everything was sorted out in good time for the expiry of the lease in July. However, as with most legal agreements, the formalities took somewhat longer, and the agreement (which actually applied from 1st July 1875) eventually materialised bearing the date of 1st June 1876.

The first part of the agreement dealt with the permanent new arrangements for running powers etc. It was stated to be 'in substitution for the (LT&SR's) powers if any under the (1852 Act)', but the fact was that the LT&SR had no existing running powers once the arrangements under the Peto Brassey & Betts lease expired. The 1876 Agreement formally and specifically granted the LT&SR running powers over the GER between Fenchurch Street and Gas Factory Junction (and was the basis on which trains ran over that section up to 1912). It is to be noted that no powers were granted into Liverpool Street via Forest Gate Junction, a subject which was to be raised more than once subsequently! £3,000 pa was to be paid in 1875/6 and 1876/7, and £4000 pa subsequently, for the use of Fenchurch Street terminus; if the station should ever need to be enlarged, it should be decided by arbitration what proportion the LT&SR should pay. For use of the line between Fenchurch Street and Gas Factory Junction, a mileage rate was to be paid for passenger traffic based on the actual mileage of two and three-quarter miles only (except for fares to Bromley and Plaistow, where the GER would get half the fare in both cases), and 9d per ton for goods traffic. (These passenger tolls were of course far more reasonable than what Peto Brassey & Betts had been forced to pay). LT&SR passenger trains could continue to call at Stepney but (as before) not at other 'L&B' stations; through bookings to continue from LT&SR stations to all stations between Fenchurch Street and Blackwall. Parcels traffic to be dealt with under normal Clearing House rules. Horse and carriage traffic from LT&SR stations to be accommodated at Liverpool Street (Fenchurch Street had never handled such traffic as the platforms could only be reached by steps).

The GER to grant through bookings between LT&SR stations and stations to Liverpool Street via Forest Gate Junction; the GER not to be obliged to run more than 4 trains per day between Liverpool Street and Barking (which presumably meant that they were now accepting an obligation to run 4) and to be paid 1s 1d per train mile by the LT&SR for the working of these trains over the Forest Gate Junction-Barking section. The GER to be entitled to run their North Woolwich trains via Bromley (they already in fact had running powers for this) paying 1s 10d per train for use of the LT&S line here, but not to stop their trains at Bromley. The GER 'when exercising their general running powers over the Tilbury line' (ie their powers under the 1852 Act, which they never exercised in practice) to pay a mileage proportion of revenue to the LT&SR.

In addition there were various provisions concerning the handling of LT&SR goods traffic in London, as described in an Appendix in Vol. 2.

All these arrangements regarding tolls could be revised after 10 years at the request of either company, so far as the rates were concerned, the question going to arbitration if necessary; but the powers granted by the agreement were permanent.

The latter part of the agreement concerned the temporary arrangements for the running of the train services by the GER. The principle of this was the same as had applied previously, ie the GER were simply to act as 'contractors' (but to the LT&SR company, instead of to Peto Brassey & Betts) supplying locomotives, stock, and traincrews. Locomotives were to be supplied for 5 years until 30th June 1880, at a charge of $10\frac{1}{2}$d per passenger train mile and 1s 2d per goods train mile (both these rates being higher than those charged to the lessees previously). Empty coaching stock and light engine movements to be charged at these same figures; engines in use for shunting to be charged at 8s per hour. Passenger trains not to exceed 18 coaches, goods trains not to exceed 30 wagons. The LT&SR to supply locomotives with water free of charge. GER employees working on the LT&S line to be considered LT&SR servants for 'rules' purposes. Carriages and Wagons to be supplied for 2 years until 30th June 1877. Up to 60 carriages and brake vans, 'to be marked London Tilbury and Southend Railway', to be provided at £50 per annum per carriage and £45 per annum per luggage/brake van. In addition, further carriages or vans to be provided (from the general GER fleet) at busy times on reasonable notice being given, at 7s 6d per day per carriage and 5s per day per luggage/brake van. 100 ordinary goods wagons and brake vans to be supplied at £13 pa, any wagons above this number, when necessary, to be at ordinary Clearing House rates.

The agreement was scheduled to the 1877 LT&SR Bill to give it parliamentary sanction. However that Bill failed, and it was never included in any subsequent Bill. This of course did not affect its validity.

The arrangement by which the GER were effectively acting as 'contractors' came to the attention of the Locomotive Manufacturers' Association and the Railway Carriage & Wagon Builders' Association, and after they won a case brought against the LNWR (who had been manufacturing locomotives for sale when this was outside their statutory powers) their solicitors wrote to the GER in March 1877 threatening to take them to court also on the basis that supplying locomotives and stock as contractors was similarly beyond a railway company's powers. This court case was proceeded with, and the Associations won in the court of first instance in January 1879, but lost in the Court of Appeal in March. The majority judgement of the Court of Appeal was that such hiring of locomotives and stock was not necessarily ultra vires merely because it was not expressly authorised, and that in any case it was specifically covered in the instant case by the 1863 Act which authorised the LT&SR to make agreements with the GER for the working of the line. The courts were influenced by the fact that the LT&SR line was so closely linked with the GER's; the GER claimed that they were not hiring stock to any other company. The House of Lords in May 1880 confirmed the Court of Appeal's judgement against the Associations.

THE TAKING OVER OF THE LINE
The LT&SR board took over the management of their line from the lessees on 1st July 1875 instead of the originally-planned 3rd July, this no doubt being agreed on the basis that it was much simpler financially for the takeover to apply from the start of the half-year. In the last 12 months of the lease, the lessees carried out a considerable amount of repair work on the line to bring everything up to the required standards for handover, and as a result their expenditure in the first half of 1875 actually exceeded the receipts. However there was still further work left after July 1875, it being noted in August that Lawford had yet to make a final report on the state of the line because of this. Nevertheless the 'handover' seems to have been arranged without dispute, a result partly, one suspects, of the fact that, with Brassey's executors now being the lessees, there was no longer any personal animosity between the parties (in addition to which, the executors were spending someone else's, rather than their own money on the extra work necessary on repairs!). On 22nd February 1876 the LT&SR Board approved the sealing of the 'mutual release' of the company and William Wagstaff and others, Executors of the late Thomas Brassey, and the lessees' role came to an end.

If the financial and legal aspects of the takeover were fundamental, the reality on the railway was one of complete continuity (save for the fact that the lessees' 'Manager' Joseph Louth had his services terminated). The GER continued running the trains. The former lessees' employees (station staff, 'selected' permanent way staff, and the few 'head office' personnel) were taken into LT&SR employment at their existing rates of pay. The lessees had been asked in January 1875 to supply a list of their staff and rates of pay, to facilitate this process.

THE NEW MANAGEMENT STRUCTURE
In April 1875 the LT&SR Board appointed Arthur Lewis Stride, formerly of the LC&DR, as 'General Manager and Resident Engineer'. He took up post immediately, quickly supplanting Underdown's role in the discussions with the GER over the agreement. Then from 1st July he took over the day-to-day management of the line in succession to Louth. He also quickly became 'Engineer', as Lawford's services were not retained once he had completed his final report on the state of the line; and in fact established himself as the lynchpin of the LT&SR organisation, a position which he retained up to 1912 without rivals.

Kennell the Company Secretary remained in office unaffected by the takeover. He was also still Secretary to the L&BR company in its residual form, which meant in practice that the GER had access to all LT&SR papers via him. Had the shareholders' directors sought his removal it is unlikely that they would have succeeded. He died in office on 1st February 1881, and was succeeded by H. Cecil Newton who was to hold the post until 1912. This saw the end of the 'Blackwall influence' in the running of the LT&SR. Kennell would naturally have seen the GER's seats on the LT&SR Board as a logical result of the line's past history. But to the 'outsiders' Stride and Newton it must have appeared an extraordinary and unacceptable nonsense;they would have wanted to run the LT&SR as a 'normal' independent railway company the same as any other, and their taking administrative control of the company must therefore have constituted another step in the gradual expunging of the GER's influence over it.

From this time on Doughty Browne, Stride and Newton were to bring a complete continuity in the running of the LT&SR through to the end in 1912.

On 28th May 1875 the Board appointed an Executive Committee to run the company, meeting weekly, with only major questions going to the full Board (for other than rubber-stamping) henceforth. This was the idea of Parkes who realised that it would be impossible to run the railway effectively by the full Board, the majority of whose members had no active interest in the undertaking. The Executive Committee initially comprised Bischoff, Doughty Browne, and Parkes, although others were added later. From 1875 to 1881 they succeeded in running the company efficiently and harmoniously, despite the underlying difficulty brought about by the GER's majority on the Board. It was not until the Tilbury Docks scheme came up in 1881 - a question where the interests of the GER and the LT&SR were too blatantly at loggerheads for harmony to continue - that a decision of the shareholders'-Directors-dominated Executive Committee was overturned by the GER-dominated full Board and conflict came to the surface again.

The Directors received only £500 pa between them in the 1870s. However the shareholders' directors were putting in considerable hours for the company and in 1881 they were granted an extra £300pa to be divided between them only.

Two Acts were obtained in 1875 to tidy up loose ends. The LT&SR (Steamboats) Act 1875 revived the company's steamboat powers which had lapsed in 1868 without anyone taking notice of the fact. The LT&SR Act 1875 authorised the abandonment of the Abbey Mills north curve and, for the first time since 1856, an increase in the company's authorised capital (£150,000 additional shares and £50,000 additional borrowing) to finance intended improvements.

Another piece of 'tidying up' was the introduction in 1875 of 3rd Class carriages on all trains (except the Southend 'expresses'), a requirement under the 1852 Act but previously flouted by the lessees. This soon resulted, as was happening all over the railway system, in 3rd class passengers becoming the great majority of the total traffic. By the mid-'80s, the LT&SR's figures were 3% 1st, 7% 2nd, and 90% 3rd.

In 1876/7 the shareholders' directors did in fact make another attempt at reforming the composition of the Board. Having discussed the matter with Parkes, Bischoff wrote to him formally in October 1876 'it seems to Mr Browne and me that the time has come when the shareholders are entitled to ask that the management of the Company should be vested in Directors elected by themselves'; and proposed a Board of 7, 4 to be elected by the shareholders, 2 by the GER and 1 by the L&BR. Parkes' response was that the GER might accept some alteration, but would need to discuss the matter further. However on 3rd November the Executive Committee (by a 2-1 majority, Parkes dissenting) resolved to include the proposed changes in the LT&SR's 1877 Bill. This was done, but the 1877 Bill was

H. (HENRY) CECIL NEWTON was born in 1853 and joined the GWR in 1869, working in the Goods Manager's office and then in the General Manager's office. In 1875 he left the GWR and went to Devon to take charge of various minor railway companies:-

Buckfastleigh, Totnes & South Devon Railway 1876-1881 Secretary

Torbay & Brixham Railway 1876-1881 Manager

Culm Valley Light Railway 1876-7 Assistant Secretary, 1877-1881 Secretary

Seaton & Beer Railway 1878-1881 Assistant Secretary

Totnes, Paignton & Torquay Direct Railway c1879-1881 Secretary

Also from 1878 he was in charge of the Railway Department of the London Financial Association, which took him back to London (but he kept the Brixham managership on the basis that he would 'visit Brixham as occasion may require'; the Secretarial posts did not really need local presence). These posts were all given up after March 1881 when he was appointed as 'Secretary and Accountant' to the LT&SR. A curious side effect was that the last meetings of the Culm Valley company were held at Fenchurch Street!

In 1889 he applied for the position of Chief Commissioner of Railways of Queensland, but was not successful.

By 1896 his LT&SR salary was £1000 pa. This was augmented by the secretaryships of the Whitechapel & Bow Railway (from February 1899 until his death), also the Tottenham & Forest Gate Railway (from November 1890 until 1914). In both cases Newton was also Secretary of the 'Joint Committee' that ran the line.

His only other office was as Auditor of the Grand Trunk Railway of Canada, from 1903.

When his main LT&SR job disappeared in 1912, Newton was 59 and does not seem to have thought it worth seeking another post. In the event he died on 4th February 1915, aged 61, and was interred in Brookwood Cemetery after a service at St Columbs, Notting Hill near his home in Kensington. The Midland Board made a donation of £1000 to his widow Catherine.

Born in 1841, ARTHUR LEWIS STRIDE was the son of Lewis Stride of Dover. He spent his earlier career in the LC&DR Engineer's department, rising by 1870 to the position of District Engineer for the Kent Coast and Sheerness district.

After coming to the LT&SR in 1875, his positions were:-

April 1875 - General Manager and Resident Engineer

c1876 - General Manager and Engineer

October 1889 - (On to the Board) Managing Director

April 1905 - Deputy Chairman and Managing Director

January 1906 - Chairman and Managing Director

His salary was £500 in 1875, but this was increased substantially when the Board realised that they had an exceptionally good Manager who might no doubt be tempted by a larger company. An increase to £1200 in 1883 was minuted 'the Board having expressed their entire approval of the energy and talent he has shown in the discharge of his duties'. By 1892 he was on £2000 and he ended up on £2900.

However he received much further income above his salary itself. Under an agreement made in January 1883, his work as Engineer for the Barking-Pitsea and Romford-Grays lines was not done as part of his employment as Manager, but separately as if he were doing it as an engineer in private practice. This led to one shareholder complaining at the July 1888 shareholders' meeting that Stride had a vested interest in the promotion of new lines.

In August 1898 he was appointed a director of the Whitechapel & Bow Railway, which he remained until 1912 having been Chairman-by-rotation of the company in some years.

In 1902 he was made a director of the Metropolitan District Railway, at an additional £1000 pa. However he had to resign this directorship in November 1906 as he had 'found he was awkwardly situated at times' when differences arose between the LT&SR and the District.

He was also on the Tottenham & Forest Gate Railway board for many years.

Stride was relieved of his responsibilities as Engineer in 1899 when J. R. Robertson was appointed as Engineer under him, and of his day-to-day responsibilities as Manager in 1907 when Benjamin Bullock (who had been Assistant Manager since 1892) was appointed Manager. Stride's last years were therefore essentially in the gentlemanly role of Chairman.

Until the late 1880s he lived at Beckenham where he had taken up residence in his LC&DR days. He then moved to Bush Hall, Hatfield, a large house beside the River Lea and adjacent to the Hatfield House estate. This was well away from the 'Tilbury'! - although convenient of course for the daily journey to Moorgate on the Great Northern.

In 1911 Stride felt the need to retire and this was one of the factors in the sale of the LT&SR to the Midland, for like many long-dominant men he had no 'successor'.

He died on 16th September 1922 at his home, after being in ill health for some time. He left £24,025 in his will. He seems to have avoided the camera, for no portraits of him appear in articles alongside those of his fellow LT&SR officers.

THOMAS WHITELEGG was born in 1840 and was a pupil and then a chargehand fitter with the locomotive builders Sharp, Stewart & Co.

He then worked for the locomotive builders Neilson's; at the Hamilton Windsor Ironworks, Garston, Liverpool, on marine engines; and with Ruston Proctor & Co, Lincoln.

He then joined the GER at Stratford works under William Adams, who was most likely the person responsible for recommending him to the LT&SR when they needed someone to look after their new locomotive fleet.

Whitelegg entered the LT&SR's service on 1st November 1879 at an initial £200 pa, becoming Locomotive Superintendent - the full title on the LT&SR was 'Locomotive Carriage Wagon & Marine Superintendent' - in April 1881 at £250, increased at various dates up to £800 pa in 1902.

In May 1910 he intimated that he wished to retire at the end of July, which he did, on a pension of £600 pa. The photograph here was taken at this time. However he died very soon afterwards in March 1911.

subsequently withdrawn owing to problems with its other main content, a Southend-Shoeburyness extension (for which see Chapter 5). As a result the idea lapsed, and the subject of changes to the Board was avoided thereafter until 1881/2.

SETTING THE SHIP STRAIGHT (1875-81)
The LT&SR line in 1875, although in reasonable condition, was a somewhat out-of-date railway. The signalling arrangements in particular were archaic for a line in the London area, with time-interval working and no interlocking (save for Bromley Junction box). This was therefore made a first target, and in 1875-8 the Block System was brought into use throughout the line, and interlocked signal boxes built at all junctions.

Unfortunately, before these improvements were effected, there was a collision at Barking in September 1875 as a result of the time-interval working. Although the rolling stock was little damaged, two passengers died and many more were injured. By the end of January 1876 no less than £14,110 had been paid out in compensation, with more to come; a very serious loss to a small company. The Board therefore decided that no dividend at all could be paid for the last half of 1875 - not a good start to the direct running of the line.

The interlocking of the remaining stations was not carried out until 1880/1. At the same time a £10,200 'package' of other station improvements - platform extensions, additional sidings, etc - was effected (after a 'tour' of the line by the Executive Committee on 9th December 1880). Also, between 1878 and 1881 the whole line was relaid with 72lb steel rails in place of 64lb iron rails.

A new station, Upton Park, was opened in 1877, the first of several additional stations to be provided under financial agreements with property developers (Chapter 9). Then in 1882/3 new and more commodious station buildings were provided at Plaistow, the original buildings having become inadequate in the face of an exploding population. This was followed by the rebuilding of Grays station in 1884.

PURCHASE OF CARRIAGES AND WAGONS
In October 1875 Stride obtained authority to order 70 coaches at an estimate of £27,850 (he had originally wanted 86). Most of these came from the Metropolitan Railway Carriage & Wagon Co, who were to become the LT&SR's most regular suppliers of both coaches and wagons for many years. The first 16 arrived in May 1876 and were put to use on the Southend 'express'; all were delivered by February 1877. Initially they had the Clarke & Webb chain brake, but the LT&SR adopted the Westinghouse air brake in 1885/6. These coaches were only sufficient for the regular daily booked service. Hiring, from the NLR and GER, continued to be necessary on peak traffic days. In July 1879 Stride sought 'another train of 3rd class carriages' which he said would make it unnecessary to hire save on very exceptional days. (Twelve carriages were destroyed when Tilbury carriage shed burnt down in July 1878, which did not help).

In February 1880 the NLR advised that they were putting 40 older coaches up for sale, and would not be able to hire after this. Stride arranged for the LT&SR to purchase these coaches. However hiring from the NLR in fact continued after this, until 1891 when the NLR changed to the vacuum brake rendering hire to the Westinghouse-braked LT&SR impossible. The LT&SR had to order a further 60 carriages in 1891 because of this. Hiring from the GER also continued after 1880. But from 1897 (when the fitting of some LT&SR locos with the vacuum brake as well as the Westinghouse brake enabled the LT&SR to hire from vacuum-brake companies) the Midland became the LT&SR's main suppliers of extra coaches on busy days. This continued until the end of the company's independent life; the Southend Bank Holiday traffic was so much above the LT&SR's regular traffic that it would have been quite uneconomic to seek to expand the LT&SR carriage fleet to accommodate it.

The first reference to the purchase of wagons is in July 1876 when Stride was authorised to acquire half a dozen from the Lancaster Wagon Co 'for vegetable traffic'. In October this order was increased to 100 10-ton opens, which the Lancaster company agreed to supply on hire purchase (a very common arrangement) at £13 18s 0d per wagon per annum for seven years.

Thus the LT&SR also had a basic fleet of goods wagons by the end of the GER hire agreement in summer 1877. But hiring of goods stock continued for some years after this. 50 more opens and 10 goods brake vans came from the Metropolitan RC&W Co in 1879, and in April 1880 they were given an order for 100 cattle trucks, to enable the hiring of cattle trucks from the GER and NLR to cease.

THE PURCHASE OF LOCOMOTIVES AND THE BUILDING OF PLAISTOW WORKS
On 30th January 1879 the Executive Committee (confirmed by the Board in February) approved Stride's plans for locomotive and carriage workshops at Plaistow (estimate £16,000) and the purchase of 12 locomotives (estimate £26,000). Stride was not a locomotive engineer and it was arranged that he would consult with William Adams, who had been Loco Superintendent of the GER until 1878 and was now with the LSWR, as to the design of the shops and the locomotives. The tender of Sharp, Stewart & Co for the locomotives, at £1,970 each, was accepted on 24th July 1879. The 4-4-2 Tank locomotives were built to a design which seems to have been evolved by the combined efforts of Stride, Adams, Sharp Stewart, and Thomas Whitelegg, who was in the GER Drawing Office at Stratford at this date (although he had, by chance, previously been with Sharp Stewart). In November 1879 Whitelegg was transferred to the LT&SR's staff as 'Chief Assistant in the Locomotive Department'; he was retitled Locomotive Superintendent in April 1881 and was to hold that post until 1910.

The first locomotive, No 1, was delivered to Stratford shed in early April 1880. By the end of June, when the GER Agreement should have ended, seven locos had been delivered; and the full twelve had arrived by the end of July. Some GER locos, therefore, were still working on the LT&S line for a short while after 30th June.

The shareholders were told in 1881 that £10,000 pa would be saved by the company using its own locomotives.

The contract for the building of the workshops was let on 24th October 1879 to Messrs Kirk & Parry of Sleaford, at £14,035. They were a sizeable firm who had done much railway work, particularly on the GNR. This was their first job with the LT&SR, but they were to have several further major contracts over the next five years, notably for the construction of the Southend-Shoeburyness and Barking-Pitsea lines, and the new station buildings at Plaistow and Grays.

The Plaistow workshops were reported 'almost completed' in August 1880, and were brought into use shortly afterwards although not fully completed until 1881. (One assumes that ad hoc arrangements had sufficed for the maintenance of the wholly new carriage and wagon fleet in the 1876-80 period). Although never described as a shed at this date, Plaistow was in fact used as a base for locomotives for traffic purposes, either from the start or from very shortly afterwards; the first clear picture comes with the 1884 Working Timetable in which it is clear that there are six locomotive diagrams based at Plaistow. This supplemented the two existing sheds at Tilbury and Southend.

Another six locomotives were delivered, to the same design, in 1881; a further twelve in 1884; and another six in 1892.

By mid-1881, therefore, the process of bringing the LT&SR up to date was completed. Dividends were rising, from 3⁵/₈% in 1876 to a maximum of 6% in 1883, now achieved on earned money. Passenger traffic was increasing quickly, not least due to the suburbanising of the area between Bromley and East Ham; and modest improvements were being made in the train services. (See Chapter 6 for details of passenger services after 1875).

It might have been thought that a period of more relaxed consolidation would follow. But this was not to be. The wholly external factor of the East & West India Dock Company's Tilbury Docks scheme in 1881 set moving a chain of events which was to result in 1882/3 in the LT&SR being rid at last of the burden of its 'GER' directors; the authorisation of a new main line to Southend; and (after 25 years in which no successful promotion at all had occurred) the fixing of the future railway map of South Essex at large.

H.C.Casserley took this view of 2149 running into Upminster with an up service on 22nd August 1926, and in the process captured (left) some of the few survivors from the original 1876 batch of 4-wheel composites seemingly in very good condition still at this date.
(H.C.Casserley).

Although taken in the 1900s, this photograph of a down train near Leigh gives a good idea of what an LT&SR passenger train of the early 1880s would have looked like. No. 1 class locos and 4-wheel stock were not used on any 'good' Southend train by this stage, so one suspects that this must be a summer extra. Although the locos had been designed to spend half their time

running bunker-first, this prescience did not extend to provision of enough lamp brackets in the right places at this end, and the usual expedient adopted, as here, was to place both the 'via Upminster' red cross on white disc, and the 'LT&SR' board, in the upper positions, the former half-obscuring the latter.
(R.M.Casserley collection).

TEN-WHEELED TANK LOCOMOTIVE FOR THE LONDON, TILBURY, AND SOUTHEND RAILWAY.

CONSTRUCTED BY MESSRS. SHARP, STEWART, AND CO., LIMITED, ENGINEERS, MANCHESTER.

(For Description, see Page 39.)

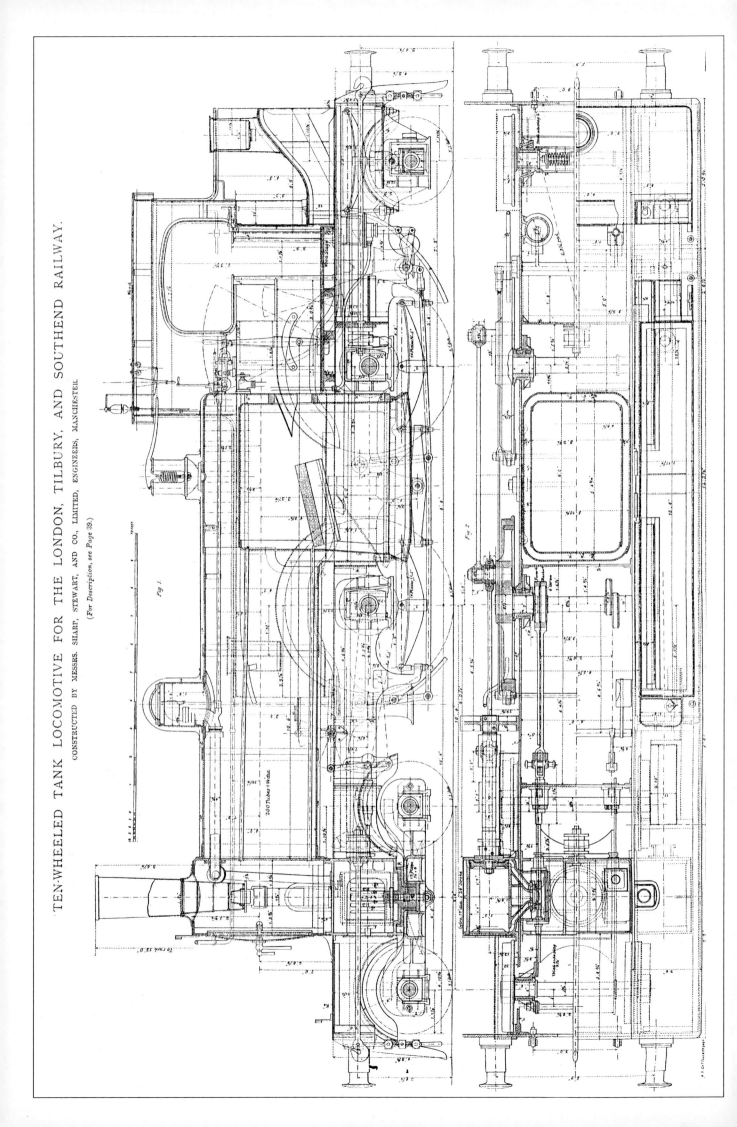

Fig. 1.

Fig. 2.

TEN-WHEELED TANK LOCOMOTIVE.

We give this week a two-page engraving, together with other views on the present page, of one of a class of ten-wheeled tank locomotives, constructed by Messrs. Sharp, Stewart, and Co., Limited, of Manchester, for the London, Tilbury, and Southend Railway. The engine is a very interesting one, not only on account of its size but also on account of certain special features in the design which deserves notice.

The London, Tilbury, and Southend Railway, although a small system, under 50 miles in length, has to deal with all the classes of traffic found upon the larger lines in this country. At Tilbury, about midway between London and Southend, two short branches run from the main line, down to, and at right angles with, the River Thames, the three lines thus forming a triangle. The ordinary stopping trains travel down one side of this triangle into Tilbury Station on the bank of the river (from which point ferry steamers run across to Gravesend), and on leaving this station by the other side of the triangle regain the main line and proceed to Southend or London. It is evident that by this operation the train is turned round during its journey, and that a tender-engine, on running round the train at Tilbury, must travel tender first for the remainder of the distance, or that a second engine must be attached to the rear of the train, which then becomes the leading end for the remainder of the journey.

The latter method is the one which has hitherto been adopted for trains stopping at Tilbury. Express trains between London and Southend run through on the straight road without going into Tilbury Station.

For many years the London, Tilbury, and Southend Railway was without any rolling stock of its own, but was worked by the Great Eastern Railway. This, however, has now been altered, and in dealing with the question of providing their own locomotive power for working the line, the engineer and manager, Mr. A. L. Stride, considered it would be a great advantage to combine in one type of engine all the capabilities for drawing the heaviest goods or cattle trains, as well as for running at high speed with expresses, and for stopping and starting quickly with ordinary passenger trains. To accomplish this satisfactorily, and to avoid the necessity for a second engine at Tilbury, Mr. Stride determined to have a tank engine that could run equally well leading or trailing end first. It was necessary, moreover, to avoid any excessive weight on any pair of wheels, and to run with freedom and safety at high speed round the frequent curves.

Compliance with conditions so varied compelled the adoption of arrangements and dimensions which are unusual and has resulted in the engine we now illustrate, which has been fitly described as a "universal machine," and which supplies the successful solution of the above-stated problem.

The engine has outside cylinders with single slide bars, and is carried in front by a four-wheeled bogie, on Mr. W. Adams's system (without, however, india-rubber or any material intervening between the upper and lower centres) in the centre by two pairs of coupled wheels 6 ft. 1 in. in diameter, and, at the trailing end, by a pair of running wheels, fitted with an arrangement of radial axle boxes designed by the makers, and which avoids the liability to jamming hitherto experienced. These axle boxes are controlled laterally, like the bogie, by coiled springs set with the degree of initial compression requisite to bring them back to the central position and to control any tendency to unsteadiness in the engine. A special feature in this arrangement is that each spring is so held that when the axle boxes leave the central position the spring on the side from which they are receding cannot follow up the movement, the effect being that immediately on the axle leaving its central position it meets with a resistance tending to return it.

The engine has 17 in. cylinders with 26 in. stroke, and the diameter of the driving wheels being as above stated, 6 ft. 1 in., the tractive power which it is capable of exerting is $\frac{17^2 \times 26}{73} = 102.9$ lb. for each pound of effective pressure per square inch on the pistons. As the coupled wheels carry a load of 32 tons 1 cwt., it will be seen that the engine has ample adhesion in proportion to its cylinder power.

The copper firebox top is stayed by direct screw bolts, a compensating arrangement being given to the two rows nearest the tubeplate, to allow of the necessary elasticity. The details have been worked out by the makers with great care, the arrangement of the radial axle-boxes presenting, as we have said, some special features which suggest their application in many instances in which bogies would ordinarily be resorted to. The engines work their trains without being turned, and run with remarkable steadiness whether with front or hind end leading. The brake arrangements consist of a steam and hand brake; the former being provided with an automatic reducing valve for regulating and reducing the pressure as may be desired. The general arrangement will be understood from the illustrations, and the dimensions will be found as under:

	ft.	in.
Cylinders and Motion:		
Diameter of cylinders	1	5
Stroke...	2	2
Distance apart between centres of cylinders	6	3
Width of steam ports	0	1$\frac{3}{8}$
,, exhaust ,, ...	0	3
Lengths of ports	1	2$\frac{1}{2}$
Diameter of piston rods	0	3
Length of connecting rods between centres	6	3
Length of eccentric rods between centres	5	8
Wheels and Frames:		
Diameter of bogie wheels	3	1
,, coupled ,, ...	6	1
,, trailing ,, ...	3	1
Distance between centres of bogie wheels	6	6
,, ,, centre of bogie and front coupled wheels	10	4
Distance between centres of coupled wheels	8	6
Distance between centres of hind coupled and trailing wheels	7	3
Fixed wheel base	8	6
Total ,, ...	29	4
Width of tyres of coupled wheels... ...	0	5$\frac{1}{2}$
,, ,, bogie and trailing wheels	0	5
Total sideplay of bogie	0	2$\frac{1}{2}$
,, ,, trailing wheels... ...	0	2
Distance apart of frames	4	0
Thickness of frames	0	1
Boiler:		
Length of barrel	10	6
Diameter of barrel inside	4	1
Thickness of barrel plates	0	0$\frac{1}{2}$
,, smokebox tubeplate ...	0	0$\frac{3}{4}$
Length of firebox shell outside	6	0
Width ,, ,, ,, at bottom	3	10$\frac{1}{2}$
Depth ,, ,, ,, below centre line of boiler	4	8$\frac{1}{4}$
Length of firebox at top inside	5	1$\frac{5}{8}$
,, ,, ,, bottom inside ...	5	4$\frac{13}{16}$
Width ,, ,, inside	3	2$\frac{3}{4}$
Height ,, ,, ,, ...	5	5$\frac{5}{8}$
Thickness of firebox shell plates, sides and back	0	0$\frac{1}{2}$
Thickness of firebox shell front plate ...	0	0$\frac{9}{16}$
,, ,, ,, top plate ...	0	0$\frac{5}{8}$
,, ,, copper plates ..	0	0$\frac{1}{2}$
,, ,, tubeplate	0	0$\frac{3}{4}$
Length of tubes between tubeplates ...	10	10$\frac{5}{16}$
Diameter of tubes outside...	0	1$\frac{3}{8}$
Number of tubes (brass) 200		
Diameter of chimney at bottom	1	3$\frac{1}{2}$

	sq. ft.
Heating surface: Tubes	923
Firebox...	97
Total ...	1020
Firegrate area	17.25
Flue area through tubes (disregarding ferrules)	2.2
Area through chimney at smallest part ...	1.31
Ratio of grate area to total heating surface	1 : 59.1
Ratio of flue area through tubes to grate area	1 : 7.84
Ratio of chimney area to grate area ...	1 : 13.17
Tanks:	
Capacity	1300 gals.

Weight in Working Order:

	tons.	cwt.	qrs.
On bogie	15	18	0
,, front coupled wheels	16	0	2
,, hind ,, ,, ...	16	0	2
,, trailing wheels	8	2	3
Total	56	1	3

Whilst it is not the purpose of this book to cover again the details of LT&SR locomotives, it was thought that this drawing from a contemporary journal might be appreciated, the more so as the accompanying text gives a good contemporary explanation of the factors considered in the design of the class. Note that the 'Universal Machine' nickname was already used at this date (1881). It will also be noted from the text that the original practice of backing all trains into Tilbury station, to avoid having to change locos or run round, had been abandoned by the late '70s, no doubt because of the hazards involved.

Fig. 3.

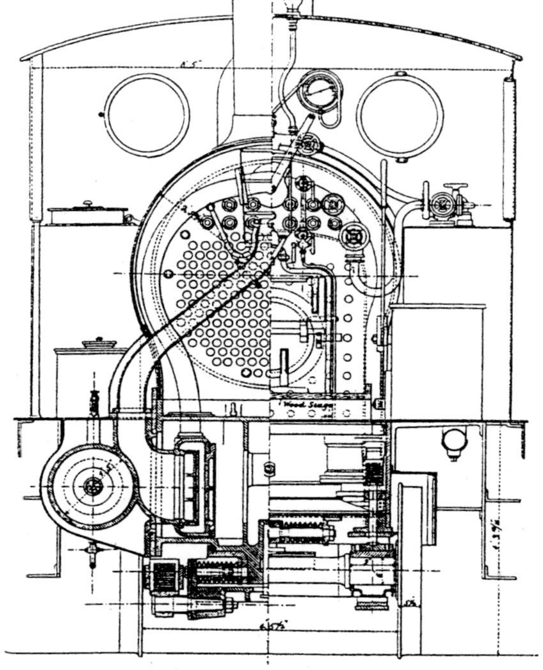

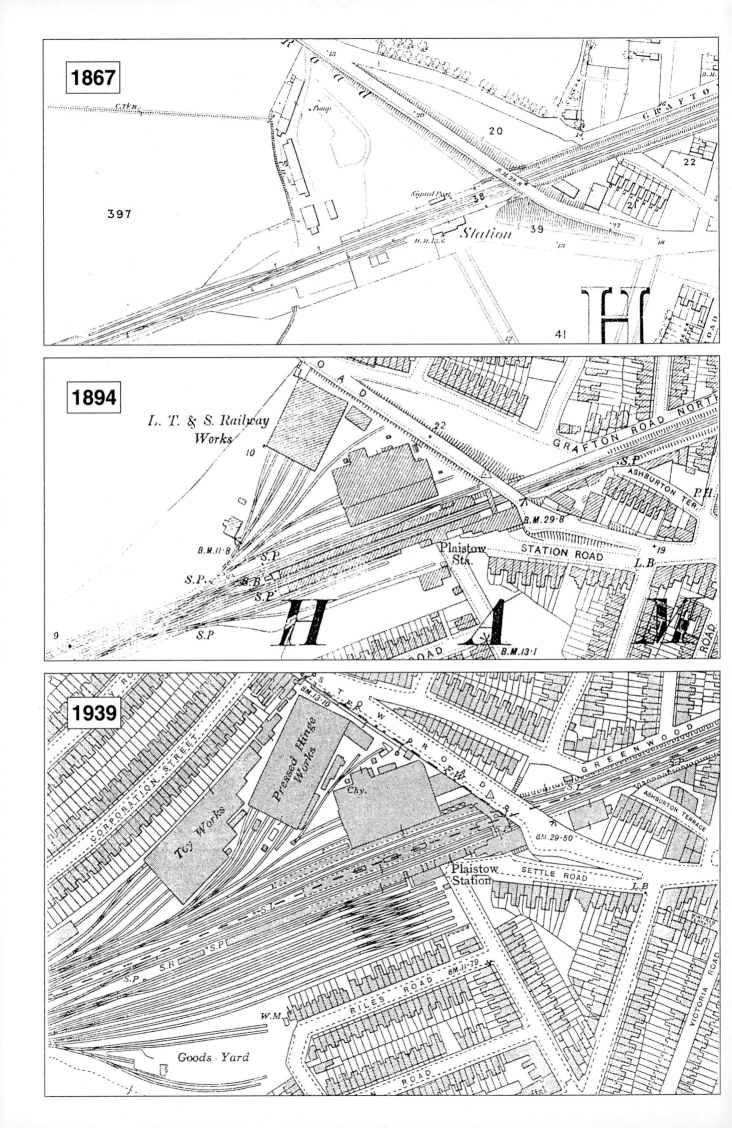

PLAISTOW STATION AND WORKS

The 1867 OS (top) shows a Plaistow still half-farmland, with the terraced streets just being laid out. The diversion of Plaistow Road effected when the railway was built stands out clearly, the old road becoming 'Grafton Road North' and 'Ashburton Terrace' on the later map. The expense of the road embankment was clearly deemed preferable to repeating the numerous level crossings on the original LT&S line of 1854-5. The 1858 station building at Plaistow, seen here, was on the up side at platform level, and passengers for down trains generally crossed the line on the level, with occasional fatal consequences. The steps up to Plaistow Road were almost certainly intended for exit only. Plaistow was a place of no particular significance originally, but from 1869 became the terminus of the NLR passenger trains, and then from 1876 the interchange point for goods traffic via the NLR. But it was the building of the Works that really 'made' Plaistow; until 1879 there was nothing on the down side except the one siding seen here.

The 1893/4 survey (centre) shows the layout of 1880, when everything was rearranged in connection with the building of the Works and an interlocked signal box was provided. The platforms were extended from 380ft to 520ft and a bay line added on the down side with runround facilities for NLR trains which had hitherto been obliged to run round on the main lines. The goods dock line behind the up platform was a survivor from the pre-1880 layout. The two sidings to the south of it are believed to have been put in 1877 for up goods traffic awaiting the NLR transfer trips.

By the 1880s the housing development of Plaistow was nearly done (although there are still some white spaces on the 1894 plan). The passenger traffic generated was swamping the original station buildings and in 1882/3 a new entrance building was provided at bridge level in Plaistow Road, with footbridge access to the down platform. A stationmaster's house was incorporated. 'Station Road' was no longer used by passengers (and was later renamed 'Settle Road' as a result). Soon after 1883 the full-length platform canopies were provided; after that nothing happened for over a decade.

The 1939 plan (bottom) shows the Plaistow of

the 1912-1950s period, as created by (1) the building of the running shed ('Toy Works' here) and enlargement of the shops in 1896-9, (2) the quadrupling of 1905 which saw the entire track layout (except the Works sidings) taken up and replaced on new alignments, including the provision of new 600ft platforms on different alignments, (3) the enlargement of the up sidings in 1912.

The 1882/3 station entrance building survived the quadrupling; it was a tight job to fit in four lines between this and the loco shops building, the south wall of which now became the back wall of the Down Local platform (having previously been two tracks clear of the station). The NLR passenger trains moved to a new bay on the south side in July 1905 and the north side bay, after seeing little use for several years, was electrified and used by terminating District trains. To give a greater available length of platform for the District trains, the Down Local/Bay platform was extended westwards in 1912. More details of how the quadrupling was done will be provided in diagrams in Vol.2.

The new goods yard off Riles Road was necessitated by the enlarged up sidings taking the site of the earlier goods accommodation.

above
The 1882 station entrance building in LMS days after insertion of a Tobacco Kiosk into the street facade. This building, which few twentieth-century eyes would consider attractive, is still in use in 1996.

below
Turning now to the Works, this painting, a photograph of which was included by Robert Whitelegg in the album he compiled in 1912, shows Plaistow Works in its original form (as in the 1894 OS extract). The 165ft by 120ft Carriage & Wagon Shop is at mid left and the 205ft by 125ft Loco Shop at right. They were built in yellow brick in a style that was to be used also for later LT&SR sheds (except the 1906 Tilbury shed). As noted in the text it is clear that the Plaistow Loco Shops were also used as a running shed for a few locos in the 1880s/90s period, and there are several locos in steam present here. The single-storey office building at far left, probably an Inspector's office, was removed in the 1890s enlargements of the Works.
(A.G.Ellis Collection).

The Plaistow facilities soon became seen as inadequate for the growing railway and the LT&SR's 1884 Act authorised the purchase of additional land to the northwest (seen fenced-off but unbuilt-on in the 1894 OS). Thomas Whitelegg submitted a report recommending expansion of the shops to the LT&SR Board in November 1893, but this was a poor period for the company financially and he had to wait. In due course Mowlem's were given contracts for £10,300 in June 1895 and £7,073 in February 1899. The main improvements were the extension of the C&W shops by 90ft southwards, and the building of a running shed (on the land bought in 1884) to get locos in traffic out of the Loco Shops building. Unfortunately it is not clear which of these two jobs was done at which date in the 1896-9 period, although the probability is that it was only in 1899 that the running shed was fully opened.

This view of the shed dates from late 1909; 79 and 81 were new in mid-1909, but 79, still in lavender-grey here, had been repainted green by 1910. Although much-photographed in the Edwardian years, this running shed lasted as such only until 1911 (it appears as 'Carriage Shops' on the works plan below, and 'Toy Works' on the 1939 OS).
(R.M.Casserley collection).

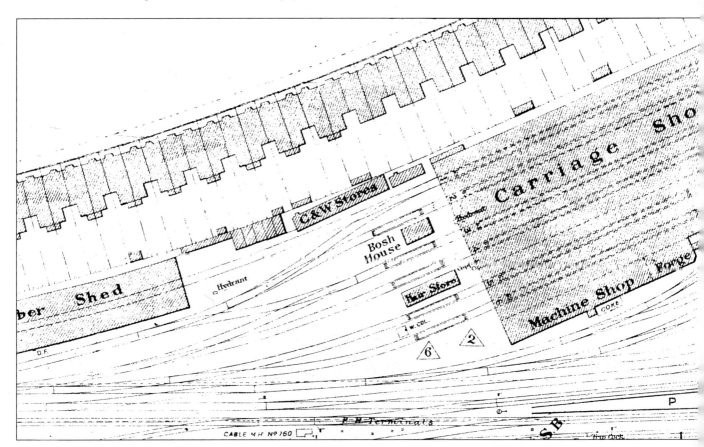

running in the peak hours made it operationally more convenient to have the running shed on the south side with direct access to the Through lines.

The LT&SR Board on 27th July 1911 approved Stride's (no doubt largely Whitelegg's) plans for the reorganising of the works following the opening of the new shed. The running shed did not need major structural alterations to convert it to its new role of C&W shops, but a Carpenters' Shop, Transformer Station and Machine Shop were added to the existing building. Mowlem's tender of £7634 for these extensions and other new buildings of which the Timber Shed (left) was the only one of note, was accepted in December 1911. The Transformer Station was in connection with a scheme for the provision of electric power and lighting for the whole works, station, and yard complex, carried out in 1912 by the British Westinghouse Electric Manufacturing Co.

The conversion of the C&W Shops to their new role as C&W Paint Shops was of course easily done.

Thus in 1912 Plaistow Works reached its final form. Its days were however soon numbered, the LMS coming to see this 'outpost' as superfluous. The Loco Shops were closed in 1925, the CME reporting to the Locomotive Committee on 17th June of that year that 'arrangements were now in hand to close down the locomotive repair shops at Plaistow, and transfer the work to the locomotive workshops at Bow on the old North London

section, it being anticipated that the transfer would be effected by the end of August'. The C&W work ended in 1931/2. The closure was agreed by the LMS C&W Committee in July 1931, on the basis of the work being transferred to Wolverton. 55 of the Plaistow staff would transfer to Wolverton and 27 be made redundant. The estimated savings were £6000 p.a. 'In anticipation of approval being given, arrangements had already been put in hand for the shops to be closed'. Much of the machinery was of course recovered for re-use elsewhere.

The buildings were let off for private industrial uses, the former C&W shops becoming a Toy Works and the former C&W Paint shops a Pressed Hinge Works, with rail access being retained for the new users. Around 1950, however, the site was let to Volkswagen and the sidings lifted. All the LT&SR buildings have now been demolished, save for part of the wall of the Coppersmith's shop on the main road and the 1880 south wall of the Loco Shops which supports the platform canopies.

(John Watling collection)

below
Plaistow Works in its (brief) heyday; the Midland 1 chain (66ft - 1 inch) survey of 1921. The building marked 'Carriage Shops' (actually C&W shops) is the former running shed of c1899 as converted; the 'C&W Paint Shops' is the 1880 C&W Shops as extended in the mid '90s (the dashed line marks the extension). The Loco Shops managed to retain the same function throughout.

The running shed of c1899 had a short life as such. It was replaced on 30th September 1911 by the new 'West Ham' shed (which, however, itself became known as 'Plaistow' after a few years) on the south side of the line west of the sewer bridge. There were two reasons for this. Firstly, extra works space was required and it was more convenient to do this by converting the shed and keeping the whole works complex together. Secondly, the frequent District trains now

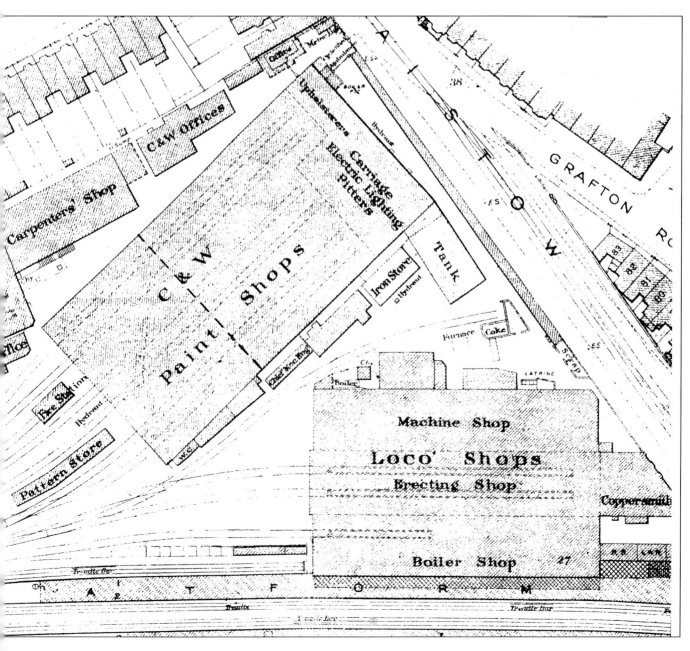

above
Photographs of the Works in their active period are few indeed. This view is dated 1912 and the Timber Shed (left) does still seem to have the shine of newness upon it. The C&W Shops (1899 running shed) sidings are full of carriages and wagons awaiting repair, as one would expect, including a couple of accident casualties in the siding by the Timber Shed. The Paint Shops (1880 C&W Shops, as illustrated in the view at page 51) are almost lost in the mist at right.
(A. G. Ellis Collection)

below
The Plaistow of the 1950s is seen in this 16th August 1958 view from the Northern Outfall Sewer bridge. Volkswagens are lined up where locos stood outside the 1899 running shed in the previous view, and the Works sidings are lifted save for a few left for engineer's use. The Works buildings themselves are still in situ here except that the chimney, and the northern two bays, of the Loco Shops have gone.

Plaistow signal box had opened in 1903, in place of the 1880 box, at an early stage in the quadrupling work. To its right is the 1905 North London Bay platform which had not been regularly used by passenger trains since the NLR service ended (and indeed the direct connection from the Down Through had been removed in 1956). The up sidings (right) were expanded to nine in 1912 after which the inner six were used as carriage sidings and the outer three as 'traffic sidings' (i.e for up goods traffic transferring to the NLR). The goods transfer function had been lost to the new Ripple Lane yard in June 1958 but the sidings are still seeing good use, for one thing and another, here. After this they were to resume an important function as carriage sidings, for midday storage of train sets, in the period between the removal of Little Ilford Southern Sidings and the electrification. The connections to the up sidings were controlled by an additional, non-block-post, signal box, Plaistow Up Sidings, opened in 1912 and just out of view at bottom left here.

This scene largely passed away in 1961/2. The up sidings were all removed and housing now occupies the site, only the names Stride Road and Whitelegg Road serving to remind one of past glories in a Plaistow where few now remain to remember the pre-1960s world.
(Frank Church, EBEG).

CHAPTER 5

Tilbury Docks and Their Consequences (1881-1886)

THE TILBURY DOCKS SCHEME

The East & West India Dock Company's situation in 1881 was far from happy. Dividends were falling, the docks were becoming inadequate as the size of steamships increased, and the rival London & St Katharine Dock Co (which had bought up Bidder's Victoria Dock in 1864) had just opened, in June 1880, the new Albert Dock which had fully up-to-date facilities for the largest ships and was accordingly attracting traffic away from the East India and West India Docks.

The choices for the East & West India Dock Co were either to modernise completely their existing docks, or to build a wholly new dock downstream. The former option was rejected on account of the disruption it would cause to traffic whilst works were in progress. Moreover, in 1881 a new company, the Thames Deep Water Dock Co, had (with the LT&SR's support) obtained powers to build a large new dock at Dagenham (reviving the 1860s ideas which had never come to fruition). This further threat could much better be combated by the East & West India Co building a new downriver dock themselves, than by any improvements to their existing docks. (In the event this Dagenham scheme too came to nothing).

The site decided upon was Tilbury. Although a radical 17 miles further downstream than any existing dock, this was not a wholly new concept. A consortium had deposited plans for a Tilbury Dock for the 1865 session, without getting beyond that stage. More significantly, August Manning the East & West India Dock Co's Engineer had himself drawn up plans for docks at Tilbury in 1867 (before he was employed by them) and presented them to Brassey, who, however, had responded that he did not wish to get involved in such large schemes at his then age, so that nothing had come of it. In 1881, however, Manning received the enthusiastic support of Col J.L. Du Plat Taylor, the Secretary and Manager of the East & West India Dock Co, for the Tilbury option.

For a time the scheme was kept quiet so that the land (all marshland) could be bought at uninflated prices. However the scheme was clearly very dependent on the co-operation of the LT&SR, and on 25th August 1881 Doughty Browne attended an 'informal meeting' at the East & West India Dock Co's offices, where 'various ideas for a traffic arrangement were put forward'. (Doughty Browne took the lead role in LT&SR affairs from this time on, as Bischoff, who was now 80, was beginning to feel his age, although Bischoff remained Chairman until January 1883). Soon after this the scheme became public, and the price of LT&SR shares, which had already increased from 122 in January 1881 to 133 in July, rocketed to 164 in October before settling in the 150s, as the market saw the company's currently-poor goods traffic increasing dramatically.

By the end of September Stride had drawn up a draft traffic agreement with the Dock Co. This was put to the LT&SR Executive Committee on 4th October and agreed. However, the full LT&SR Board, after lengthy discussions on 6th and 20th October, refused to confirm it. The primary reason for this was that the GER had all the traffic from the Victoria and Albert Docks and did not wish to see dock traffic now diverted to the LT&SR instead, so the 'GER' Directors were all against. There had already been some strain in GER/LT&SR relations of late - in 1880 the GER had enticed the United Steamship Co of Denmark away from Thames Haven to Harwich, and in summer 1881 the GER were trying to undercut the Southend tripper traffic with a rival rail/steamer facility via Blackwall - but these were relatively minor matters by comparison with the Tilbury scheme, which brought the whole question of the GER

and L&BR Directors' positions on the LT&SR Board to a head within days. Bischoff took independent legal advice, and on 22nd November 1881 a special shareholders' meeting was held at which it was resolved (with only Parkes dissenting) that clauses should be included in the LT&SR's 1882 Bill seeking alterations in the Board to remove the GER majority. The meeting also appointed a 'Committee of Shareholders' to act with the three shareholders' directors in the promotion of the Bill; and they on their own responsibility used the company's seal to make the application to parliament.

Things were also moving on other fronts. The LT&SR had already been planning an 1882 Bill for a **Southend-Shoeburyness Extension.** This was no new idea. Peto had announced in June 1855 that he 'contemplated extending the line from Southend to Shoeburyness for the convenience of Government with whom he was in communication on the subject' ('Government' meaning the Army's Shoeburyness artillery ranges, set up in 1849/50). It is probable that the military were negative , as five months later Peto was obliged to state that the scheme was given up. Then there had been the independent Rochford Hundred Railway (1866) and Southend & Shoeburyness Railway (1868) schemes, both nugatory. In 1876 the LT&SR had taken up the bit again itself, and deposited parliamentary plans for the 1877 session. A communication was sent to the Secretary of State for War in November 1876 'calling his attention to the advantages' (in transporting men and materials to the artillery camp), but only produced a hostile response on the grounds of supposed 'effects' on the establishment. The Bill was proceeded with, nonetheless, in the hope of changing the War Office's mind before the parliamentary committee stage; but they would not be budged to a more logical position and, as it was deemed futile to fight the Secretary of State in parliament, the LT&SR decided in March 1877 that the Bill must be withdrawn.

In 1881 intimations were received that the War Office were now favourable, and with another independent 'Southend & Shoeburyness' scheme being got up (this was given up when the LT&SR went ahead themselves), the LT&SR felt that the time had come to act. Stride was told to prepare plans on 13th October, and a week later a letter from Col Deeds, Undersecretary for War, confirmed the support of the military.

More importantly, the LT&SR had also been giving a rather preliminary consideration to the idea of a **cut-off line from Barking to Pitsea.** The emergence of the Tilbury Docks scheme quickly transformed this into an immediate project, as it was foreseen that the Tilbury Docks goods traffic would congest the Barking-Tilbury section to the extent that the Southend traffic would need to be kept clear of it. (Quadrupling from Barking to Tilbury was also considered as an alternative, or in addition). Another factor, one suspects, was that once it became clear in October/November 1881 that the GER and LT&SR were likely to become 'divorced' within the year, the LT&SR saw the desirability of doing something to 'claim' the country in between. At any rate, Stride was authorised on 22nd September 1881 to 'put in hand a survey for a direct line from Barking to Pitsea, with a view to this being deposited in the next session should the Board think it desirable'. After an attempt by some to go for a cheaper Rainham-Stanford-le-Hope cut-off instead - an idea which Stride was rightly opposed to on the grounds that the country on such a line would be much less likely to attract residential development and produce a local traffic - this was confirmed on 13th October. (The LT&SR were now setting eyes on Hornchurch and Upminster as potential sources of 'good' residential traffic).

Thirdly, the anticipated Tilbury Docks goods traffic made it necessary for the LT&SR to consider the provision for the first time of its own goods station in central London, in place of the use of GER depots as hitherto. This resulted in plans for a **goods station at Commercial Road** off the Fenchurch Street line, incorporating warehouses for the Dock Co's use.

The 'Shareholders' Committee' met regularly between December 1881 and July 1882 to see to the progress of these schemes and the proposed East & West India Dock Co agreement. Stride and Newton co-operated with the Committee, against the Board at large; they had the same interests, and it soon became clear that the wind was blowing in the shareholders' directors' favour and against the GER directors. One of the Committee's more pleasant happenings was an outing on 7th January 1882 when they took a special train to Barking 'and drove thence via Hornchurch and Upminster to the summit of Laindon Hill for the purpose of inspecting the proposed Barking and Pitsea line, returning subsequently to town by special train from Stanford-le-Hope'. On the 14th they had a similar trip to Shoeburyness.

The Tilbury Docks agreement will be returned to later in the Chapter. In the meantime we must consider how the LT&SR fared in the exciting parliamentary sessions of 1882 and 1883 - the most important in its history.

THE SESSION OF 1882
The 1882 session saw no less than seven bills directly affecting the LT&SR. These were:-

1 The **LT&SR** Bill for the changes in the Board to remove altogether the GER and L&BR directors, and for the new Barking-Pitsea, Southend-Shoeburyness, and Commercial Road lines; also to authorise the £600,000 additional share capital and £200,000 additional borrowing needed to finance those lines. The Bill was naturally opposed by the GER and L&BR, and by the Romford & Tilbury (see below), as well as incurring the usual objections from some landowners; but in the circumstances it had a comparatively easy ride in Committee (the Romford & Tilbury were excluded in the House of Lords on the grounds that they had themselves argued in the Commons that their scheme and the LT&SR's were complimentary rather than conflicting). In contrast to the experiences of 1874 and 1877, the wish to be rid of the GER and L&BR directors was on this occasion received sympathetically. The Act received the Royal Assent on 24th July 1882 and the LT&SR became, at last, a 'normal' independent railway company.

2 The **East & West India Dock Co's** Bill for the Tilbury Docks. This too had a fairly easy ride for such a scheme, the only major opposition coming from the Thames Deep Water Dock Co who were promoting the rival Dagenham Docks scheme. The Act was passed on 3rd July 1882.

3 The **Thames Deep Water Dock Railway** Bill. This was their response to events. The LT&SR had supported them in 1881 when they promoted their Bill for the dock itself, but when the Tilbury scheme came along the LT&SR had effectively 'ditched' the Thames Deep Water Dock Co in favour of Tilbury. They, therefore, promoted this 1882 Bill for a railway to be built by them from the GER at Custom House to the Dagenham Docks, so that they would not be dependent on the LT&SR. The GER themselves denied any involvement, perhaps truthfully. In any case the Bill was rejected.

4 The **Romford & Tilbury Railway** Bill. This was an independent scheme, designed to give the GER access to Tilbury Docks; it did secure the GER's support and an offer to work it. (The GER made no attempt to oppose the Tilbury Docks scheme itself, much as it may have wished to; the tide was too much in favour of it, and the securing of a GER link to the new docks was seen as the more positive option). The 'Romford & Tilbury Railway' seems to have been evolved by the Engineer Lionel H. Shirley, who had been brought into the area in 1881 to survey the Romford Canal (partly-built following an 1875 Act) and form an estimate for its completion. When the Tilbury Docks scheme became public in September 1881, Shirley diverted his attentions to the drawing up of the Romford & Tilbury Railway as a speculative venture of his own. He put it to the major landowners of the area, who were almost all in favour, seeing it as giving them better access to Romford market.

Shirley proposed a double-track railway, estimated at £245,407. At the south end of the line there was to be a connection to the LT&SR plus a branch running directly into the docks. Running powers were sought over the LT&SR into Tilbury station.

The Romford & Tilbury was considered in April 1882 by the same House of Commons committee, under Sir Wilfrid Lawson, that was dealing also with the LT&SR Bill. Leading evidence was given by two of the intended Directors, Sir Thomas Barrett-Lennard of Belhus and Col Champion Russell of Stubbers, North Ockendon (the latter admitting 'I know nothing about railway matters'!), followed by the usual selection of other landowners and traders. Also a witness was Thomas Bird, Chairman of

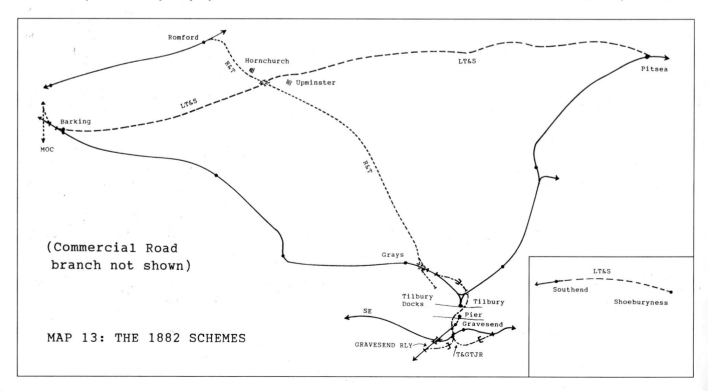

(Commercial Road branch not shown)

MAP 13: THE 1882 SCHEMES

the Romford Local Board, which had resolved in favour of the scheme. Romford market was the main South Essex market, held on Wednesdays, primarily for stock and corn; but those living in 'LT&S' territory could only reach it by road or by a special omnibus that ran from Rainham station on Wednesdays. Reference was also made to the new railway enabling farmers to bring in manure more cheaply for market gardening (ie stable manure, at present brought by river to Rainham Creek). All this of course was fairly typical of the sort of evidence that was regularly put for railway schemes in parliament - oblivious to the obvious fact that the traffics in question were nowhere near enough to provide a return on the capital costs of building a railway line.

William Birt, the GER General Manager, told the Committee that the GER had given an undertaking to work the line (although there was no legal agreement). The LT&SR was the only serious opponent, Stride's evidence being angled primarily towards showing that there was insufficient traffic potential to justify the line.

The Romford & Tilbury was passed by the Commons committee. However, it was thrown out by the Lords on financial grounds.

5 The **Tilbury and Gravesend Tunnel Junction Railway** Bill. This was passed, making it the second 'Thames Tunnel' scheme to succeed in parliament, following the London Essex & Kent Coast Junction Railway of 1876 which (Chapter 3) had subsequently fizzled out so leaving the field open again. The T&GTJR was another independent speculative scheme by financiers, working with the well-known Edinburgh-based contractor John Waddell (who had built the Mersey Tunnel). The Engineers were A.L. Nimmo and C. Minns. The LT&SR took a backseat approach to the scheme, Doughty Browne telling the shareholders that 'he did not think that it would do them harm, but what the good might be he did not know'. There is no reason to think that there was any connection with the 'Romford & Tilbury'; the people involved were all different, and had there been any link it would surely have been arranged for the two lines to meet directly instead of having a short stretch of LT&S line between their endpoints. The T&GTJR's Act gave the LT&SR running powers over the line, and also required them to compensate the LT&SR for any lost ferry traffic.

A prospectus was produced in 1883, but no money was ever raised and an Abandonment Act was obtained in 1885.

6 The **Gravesend Railway** Bill. The Gravesend Railway itself, from the LC&DR main line at Fawkham to a terminus in West Street, Gravesend, had been authorised by an 1881 Act. The Gravesend Railway was essentially a child of the LC&DR. The 1882 Bill now sought a very short extension of the line on to a new pier to be built in the Thames. The LT&SR were hostile to this, seeing it as abstracting steamboat and 'tendering' traffic from Tilbury. However the Act was passed. (The line opened in 1886, and did attract some steamboat traffic, enabling the LC&DR to carry passengers from London to the Essex resorts to a modest extent; also from 1916 to 1939 the Batavier Line ran a Rotterdam service from this pier).

7 The **Metropolitan Outer Circle Railway** Bill. The MOCR was to run from the GWR at Ealing Broadway to the GER at Custom House, connecting with most of the lines crossed en route, including the LT&SR at Barking West Junction. The LT&SR made an agreement under which the MOCR would have running powers from Barking to Tilbury, and the LT&SR running powers over the MOCR. The MOCR got its Act but proved to be yet another grand speculative scheme which failed to materialise.

The LT&SR therefore came out of this busy session very well. Its own Bill was passed in its entirety; the Tilbury Docks Bill was passed; and two of the three 'hostile' Bills were rejected. The passing of the Gravesend Railway's Bill was, by comparison, only a very trivial matter.

THE NEW LT&SR BOARD

The 'GER' and 'L&BR' directors made their last appearance at the 6th July 1882 Board meeting. The 1882 Act stipulated that the number of directors henceforth should be between 5 and 7 (in the Bill as originally presented, it had been proposed that the East & West India Dock Co should appoint a further 2 directors to the LT&SR Board, but this had been withdrawn). The half-yearly shareholders' meeting, held, one week after the passage of the Act, on 1st August 1882, elected four new directors to supplement the existing three 'shareholders' directors (Bischoff, Doughty Browne, and John Turner). Those elected were William Ford, Henry Oxenham, and James Hall Renton, who had all been on the 1881/2 'Committee of Shareholders'; and Thames Wrake Ratcliff who had originally come on to the Board as an L&BR representative but had since become a shareholder and taken an active interest. Under the 1882 Act the directors were required to hold £1,000 of shares.

The Board henceforth met every two weeks and took the full management of the company's affairs, the 'Executive Committee' being abolished. The temporary 1881/2 'Committee of Shareholders' was also abolished.

(In 1885 a 'Works Committee' and a 'Stores and Traffic Committee' were set up to relieve the full Board, but both of these were abolished in 1887, after which there were no committees until 1905 when a 'Finance Committee' was established. There was also a temporary 'Whitechapel Committee' in 1884/5 for the building of the Commercial Road depot, and a temporary 'London Tilbury & Southend Railway and East & West India Dock Co Joint Committee' in 1885/6).

Work began on the construction of the Tilbury Docks straight away in July 1882; on the Southend-Shoeburyness line in late 1882; and on the Barking-Pitsea line in late 1883. These are all discussed in detail later.

THE SESSION OF 1883

There was no let-up in the parliamentary activity in 1883, both the LT&SR and the GER seeing a need to promote further new lines. The GER wanted a line to Southend, now that it had 'lost' the LT&S line, and decided on the Shenfield-Billericay-Wickford-Rayleigh-Rochford route (which had of course been suggested on previous occasions). In fact Wilson the GER Engineer had been asked late in 1881 to survey such a line for the 1882 session, but had been unable to do the work in time due to the difficulty of the country traversed. When they became aware of the GER ideas, the LT&SR in the summer of 1882 evolved a rival Pitsea-Rayleigh-Rochford-Southend 'loop' which was of course essentially a 'block line'.

Secondly the GER wanted a Romford-Tilbury line, to give them the access to the Tilbury Docks which they had failed to secure in 1882 via the independent 'Romford & Tilbury'. The LT&SR saw a need to promote their own rival 'block' scheme to this also.

In September 1882 there were meetings between Stride and Birt the GER General Manager, and between Doughty Browne and Parkes, to see if any 'mutual understanding' could be come to to avoid the expense of parliamentary conflict. On 12th October Stride told the LT&SR Board that it had now been agreed between him and Birt that the GER should build the Romford-Upminster and Shenfield-Rayleigh sections, and the LT&SR the Upminster-Tilbury and Pitsea-Rayleigh-Southend sections. At this point, Parkes approached Doughty Browne with the proposition that the GER might take over the LT&SR altogether - no new idea of course! - but the first time it had been aired since 1875. The LT&SR Board made it clear that they might consider this, but at a special meeting on 9th November 1882 they rejected the GER's offer as inadequate. (The LT&SR was now paying 6%, making it difficult for the less-profitable GER to make a good offer). The GER had hoped to get agreement on a takeover in time for it to be included in the 1883 GER Bill, but this was now defeated by the clock, and in December Parkes stated that 'negotiations were at an end for the present'.

The negotiations over the new schemes also went wrong in November. Stride found Birt making new demands instead of discussing detail (one suspects this was because the agreed plan

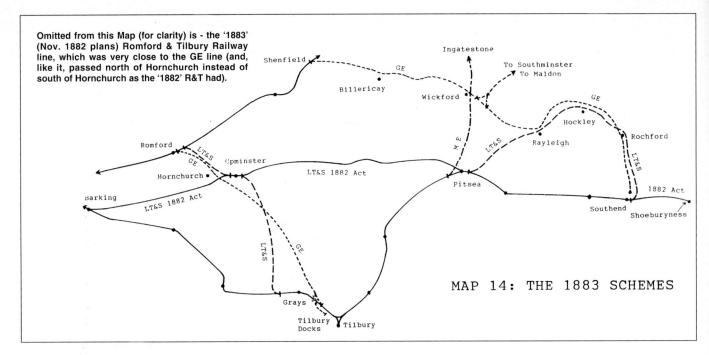

Omitted from this Map (for clarity) is - the '1883' (Nov. 1882 plans) Romford & Tilbury Railway line, which was very close to the GE line (and, like it, passed north of Hornchurch instead of south of Hornchurch as the '1882' R&T had).

MAP 14: THE 1883 SCHEMES

of October, which had been rather a concession by Birt insofar as it kept the GER out of both Tilbury and Southend, had been overruled by others in the GER). The 30th November parliamentary deadline was now imminent, and both parties were accordingly obliged to deposit plans for their full rival schemes. The GER plans included lines through rather uneconomic country to Southminster and Maldon, to 'fill in' gaps in the map in an area where LT&SR-based anti-GER moves had of course been made in the past.

Shirley's independent 'Romford & Tilbury' was also redeposited for the 1883 session with minor route alterations, but was not proceeded with in parliament once it became clear that one of the other schemes for the corridor would go ahead. Also deposited for 1883, but again not proceeded with, was an independent 'Mid Essex Railway' from Ingatestone to Pitsea.

Doughty Browne and Parkes had another meeting in December 1882, but whilst both sides agreed on the desirability of an agreement, no agreement proved possible. The LT&SR were distinctly unenthusiastic over their Romford-Tilbury line (the LT&SR scheme as finalised actually joined the existing line west of Grays). Doughty Browne noted at the February 1883 half-yearly meeting that 'he looked with great reluctance on spending money which per se was not likely to give a return. It was hardly possible in these agricultural lines to get such a return as would meet the interest on the capital' and again in July 'as a local line it would not make a very good return, but it would give them an alternative route to the docks ... it was desirable to get the line because it would give them control of the Tilbury traffic'.

The GER were similarly rather muted in their enthusiasm for the Southminster and Maldon lines.

On 1st March 1883 there was a full-scale meeting of the two companies' directors and officers at Liverpool Street in a final attempt to secure some agreement before the parliamentary committee stage, but again in vain. The now-inevitable contest therefore began, with a lengthy Commons Committee hearing between 24th April and 4th May. Both Bills were considered by the same Committee under Sir John Ramsden, the GER's first.

The Committee made it clear that they were unfavourable towards the GER's Romford-Tilbury line, so when the LT&SR came to give evidence for their Romford line they were put in the position of having to justify a local traffic need for it, an embarrassing reversal of the situation of twelve months earlier when they had been attacking the independent 'Romford & Tilbury' on the grounds that there was no real traffic demand! Counsel for the GER naturally made much of the fact that the LT&SR line was really only being promoted for blocking purposes. Fortunately the major local landowners had come out in favour of the LT&SR, Sir Thomas Barrett-Lennard and Col

Russell, who had both been pro-'R&T' the year before, now giving evidence for the LT&SR (which was perfectly reasonable on their part, given that the 'R&T' had been the only option in 1882). The Romford Local Board, however, had decided to back the GER. Stride also gave evidence that the line - which was planned as double track at this stage - would enable some freight traffic for Tilbury docks to run via Upminster, so avoiding the need to quadruple the Barking-Tilbury section; a reason which had also been used the year before to justify the Barking-Pitsea line. (In the event, thanks to poor traffic, there was never any need to run Tilbury goods trains via Upminster). At any rate, the LT&SR succeeded in getting the Committee to approve their Romford line.

In contrast, the Committee gave distinct hints that they were unimpressed by the LT&SR's Pitsea-Rayleigh-Southend loop line, and the case for this was only put half-heartedly.

Much of the Committee's time was taken up with a further aspect of the LT&SR's Bill, the seeking of running powers into Liverpool Street. It will be recalled that the LT&SR had sought such powers previously in 1874 to no effect; the raising of the question again now was probably due to the fact that Liverpool Street, with its 'Underground' connections, was coming to be seen as the more desirable terminus, whereas Fenchurch Street (which had been regarded as the best-sited station in London in the 1850s) was gradually receiving the mantle of the 'inconveniently connected' station. The existing service of 4 trains per day between Liverpool Street and Barking, for connections into LT&SR trains, was in reality all but useless as a means of giving LT&SR passengers access to Liverpool Street. Doughty Browne went so far as to offer the GER running powers over the Barking-Pitsea line in exchange for LT&SR powers into Liverpool Street (albeit that this may have been two-edged, in the hope that it might bring the Committee to reject the GER's Shenfield-Southend line on the basis that they could run via Laindon instead!).

On 1st May the Committee proposed a 'compromise' under which the GER would give the LT&SR powers into Liverpool Street, and the LT&SR would withdraw their Pitsea-Rayleigh-Southend line. The GER (rightly) rejected this. After further consideration the Committee then decided in favour of all the GER lines (except Romford-Tilbury), and against the LT&SR Pitsea-Rayleigh-Southend line. The approval of the GER lines was under the proviso that the Wickford-Southend section could not be opened until the Southminster and Maldon lines were already open - it being suspected that the GER might otherwise never build the latter lines. The LT&SR's application for running powers into Liverpool Street was rejected, but a clause was added to the Bill obliging the GER to run eight trains per day from Liverpool Street to Barking including through coaches to

Southend LT&S.

The House of Lords Committee did not alter any of this. (The LT&SR's Counsel proposed that the LT&SR should be given running powers over the GER's Southend line, via a connection to be built between the Southend stations under a future Bill, so that passengers from that line would have convenient access to the LT&SR system; but this was rejected). The GER Act was passed on 16th July 1883 and the LT&SR Act on 20th August.

The LT&SR therefore came out of the 1883 session much less well than they had in 1882. The GER had got their Act for the rival Southend line which was bound to affect the LT&SR's revenue; and they themselves were saddled with having to build the uneconomic Romford line. The only wry pleasure available was that the GER were lumbered with building the even more uneconomic Maldon and Southminster lines. Such was the British way of railway system planning.

The 1884 session seemed set to be as exciting as the previous two, with a joint LT&SR/Metropolitan Bill being promoted for a line from Whitechapel to Bromley. However, this Bill (which is discussed further in Chapter 8) was withdrawn, and after this the LT&SR had a relatively quiet time parliamentarily until the end of the 1880s.

THE BUILDING OF TILBURY DOCKS

The Dock company's hopes of getting an agreement sealed with the LT&SR before they went to Parliament were frustrated by the dissension on the LT&SR Board. In the event the agreement was only formalised in November 1883. The major provisions were -

- The LT&SR to build an additional station near Tilbury 'to be called the Dock station'.
- The LT&SR to construct a junction with the Dock railway system (i.e. Tilbury Dock North Junction) and the Dock company to make exchange sidings.
- The LT&SR to run 'a liberal train service' between Fenchurch Street and Tilbury between 9am and 7pm, calling at the new Dock station. This to include two trains an hour between 9am and 3pm down and between 11am and 5pm up, one of the two to be fast and timed in not more than 40 minutes between Fenchurch Street and the Dock station. (But after a 'fair trial' the LT&SR could give notice to the Dock company that they would withdraw any train earning less than 2s6d per train mile). The ordinary fares not to exceed 2s 1st, 1s6d 2nd, 1s 3rd single, and 2s6d 1st, 2s 2nd, 1s6d 3rd return. Season tickets to be available Tilbury-London for any of the Dock company's 'clients' at £12.10s per annum 1st class, £9 per annum 2nd.
- Special passenger trains to be run as required for ships, at the usual special train rates.
- The LT&SR to provide a London goods depot for docks traffic at Commercial Road, and construct a warehouse there for the Dock company's use. The charge for all goods between London and Tilbury to be 4s6d per ton, with a guarantee of 200,000 tons per annum. (This was to result in many years of haggling when the dock traffic fell far below expectation).

No time was lost by the Dock company in starting work on the dock, a sod-cutting ceremony taking place on 8th July 1882 only five days after the Act was passed. The contractors were Kirk & Randall but they got into difficulties in 1884 and work stopped for a time; a new contract was given to Lucas & Aird in October 1884. By the time the works were completed in 1886 the cost had reached £2,800,000 instead of the estimated £1,100,000.

The opening ceremony was held on Saturday 17th April 1886. But the great hopes that the LT&SR and the East & West India Dock Company had of Tilbury soon proved to be wildly overoptimistic. Traffic was at a very low level in the first years after 1886, and the 'minimum' rail traffic of 200,000 tons was not reached until 1903. Even when the dock (which had really been built before its time) became a success, much of the traffic went upriver in lighters and not by rail. A detailed account of the railway's dock traffic at Tilbury will appear in a future work.

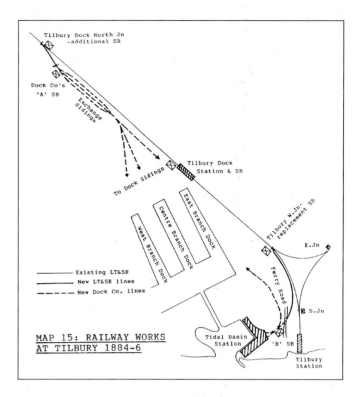

MAP 15: RAILWAY WORKS AT TILBURY 1884-6

—————— Existing LT&SR
———— New LT&SR lines
- - - - - New Dock Co. lines

The major works actually carried out by the LT&SR in consequence of the dock agreement were

-The new passenger station 'Tilbury Dock' (which was often to be called 'Tilbury Docks' in practice, no definite policy ever emerging). This opened as bare platforms around May 1884 for a Workmen's service from Grays, and for public passenger traffic on 17th April 1886, the same day as the dock itself.

-The main connection to the dock railway system at 'Tilbury Dock North Junction' where a new signal box was provided. This was a simple enough job on flat marshland.

-The secondary connection to the docks railway system, from Tilbury West Junction to the Tidal Basin station.

Maj.Gen. Hutchinson inspected all these Tilbury works in early April 1886, and noted that the Dock company had not put their section of the Tidal Basin branch (west of Ferry Road level crossing) up for inspection at all. When he came back to inspect it later in the month he was dissatisfied on several accounts but it had already been brought into use!

-The Commercial Road depot and warehouses. This was by far the biggest job. The contract went to Mowlem who could not commence until late 1884 as the details were altered, requiring a reapplication to parliament in 1884. The goods depot was ready for use in April 1886 but the warehouses were not handed over to the Dock company until August 1887.

LIVERPOOL STREET SERVICES

Since the diversion of 'LT&S' trains to the Gas Factory Junction - Barking line on 31st March 1858, the ECR/GER had run a service of 4 trains per day from Bishopsgate (Liverpool Street from 1875) to Barking, to maintain a service over that section. The 1876 GER/LT&SR agreement provided that the GER were not obliged to run more than 4, but Stride subsequently asked for more, to no avail. The LT&SR were also being asked by the public for a station in the Little Ilford/Woodgrange Park area, but there was no point in providing one so long as this limited service prevailed. Not surprisingly the infrequent service was little used. An 1860 Accident Report notes that the train had only three coaches, and usage in 1882 was reported to be less than in 1876. The July 1883 timetable, reproduced in Chapter 6, shows how poor most of the connections at Barking were, and how unlikely the service was to be used as a Liverpool Street-Southend facility.

THROUGH COACHES (1883).
s.28 of the LT&SR Act 1883 required the GER to run 8 trains per day (it actually said 'not exceeding' 8, a rather odd wording; what was meant was that there was no obligation to run more than 8) between Liverpool Street and Barking, containing through coaches to Southend which were either to be attached to trains ex-Fenchurch Street at Barking or worked through separately. This new service was introduced in October 1883, and the June 1884 LT&SR WTT here gives full details. In fact all the through coaches were always attached to Fenchurch Street trains rather than run through separately, so they actually ran to Shoeburyness. Only the LT&SR coaches ran through; the GER coaches only went to Barking and came back on a different working earlier (hence also the one ECS train here). In

one or two cases, though, it is specified that a 'GE brake' works through. The trains called at all stations between Liverpool Street and Barking, save for the 5.32pm which was put on as a 'residential express' and ran non-stop (with, it was later reported, an average load of five passengers!). On Sundays there were only three trains from Liverpool Street and no through coaches.

REDUCTION TO SIX TRAINS (1885).
Although this service was a considerable improvement, it was unfortunately not supported by the public, and in 1885 it was reduced to six trains each way (the withdrawn trains were the 6.18, 8.54 and 5.32/6.2 down and the 8.16 and 2.28 up). Indeed in 1884/5 the LT&SR several times considered withdrawing the through coaches altogether, although this was not done. The exact timings naturally varied over the years. From 1888 most of the through coaches were on trains via Laindon, but some still went on Tilbury trains.

RESTORATION OF EIGHT TRAINS (1892).
In the competition for Southend traffic that followed the opening of the GER route in 1889, the LT&SR became keen on a better Liverpool Street-Southend LT&S service again. (Indeed, in 1891 they made another attempt at getting running powers into Liverpool Street, as described in Chapter 6). Accordingly, the Barking service was restored to eight trains again in 1892, all still with through LT&SR coaches to Southend (or Tilbury). From 1894 the trains called additionally at Woodgrange Park. The 1897 GER WTT shows that they all used Platform 18 at Liverpool Street on weekdays, a suitably obscure part of the station!

WITHDRAWAL OF MOST THROUGH COACHES (1897).
The realities of underuse, however, revealed themselves again. Now that the GER had its own services to Southend, it was even less likely that passengers from the

GE line would use this less frequent 'LT&S' service. It is stated by H. V. Borley that the running of through coaches ceased as from 1.7.1897; the GER public timetables have the reference to through coaches deleted as from the November 1897 edition, which can probably be taken as confirming Borley's date.* The 8 GER trains between Liverpool Street and Barking were maintained, and they continued to have some LT&SR coaches in the train sets, even though these coaches did not now run through to Southend. Ken Nunn, writing in 1952, recalled his childhood experience of these coaches c 1900:-

'a couple of LT&SR 4 wheelers (usually very dilapidated) were attached to the GER trains, and as the Barking roster involved trips to other suburban stations during the day, these two vehicles could be sampled anywhere between Liverpool Street, Loughton and Chadwell Heath, but they never went beyond. My brother and I usually made a dive for these vehicles ...'.

END OF THE GER BARKING SERVICE (1918).
The Barking service remained at 8 per day until 1915 when wartime economies saw it cut to 6. It was then withdrawn entirely on 1.5.1918. The 1921 GER timetable still shows it as 'suspended', but it was never resumed after the war ended. The Forest Gate Junction-Woodgrange Park Junction section was thereby 'closed' to passenger traffic, until 1968 when the practice of running late night LT&S line trains from Liverpool Street was initiated.

Additionally, the LT&SR ran P&O Boat Trains to Liverpool Street.

*However, the 1908 LT&SR WTT (the first post-1897 WTT available) in fact shows a residual one train each way with through coaches to and from Shoeburyness on weekdays. This was probably kept to maintain the principle more than to benefit real passengers!

WORKING TIMETABLE JUNE 1884
Liverpool Street services.

DOWN

							SX	SO		
Liverpool St.	6.18am	8.5am	8.54am	11.26am	2.10pm	4.8pm	5.32pm	6.2pm	7.36pm	9.31pm
Barking arr.	6.44	8.31	9.20	11.52	2.37	4.35	5.50	6.28	8.2	9.57
dep.	6.56	8.48		12.6pm	2.52	4.46	6.5	6.41	8.11	10.11
Southend	8.13	10.12		1.30	4.15	A	7.5	8.5	9.35	B

UP

Southend	C	8.00am	11.30am	D	2.5pm		5.30pm	7.25pm	F
Barking arr.	8.7am	9.17	12.52pm	2.22pm	3.24		6.52	8.37	10.12pm
dep.	8.16	9.22	12.57	2.28	3.29	4.45pm	7.0	8.54	10.18
Liverpool St.	8.42	9.48	1.23	2.56	3.55	E	7.27	9.21	10.46

Notes:	A To Tilbury 5.19pm	B To Tilbury 10.44pm	C From Tilbury 7.35am
	D From Tilbury 1.50pm	E ECS to Stratford	F From Tilbury 9.40pm

---

right

Shoeburyness in the 1900s. There are no known views of the buildings prior to 24th December 1890 when 'considerable damage' was caused by a fire starting in the lamp room, but it appears, from the lack of any references to new buildings, that the 1884 buildings were restored in their original form after the fire, and that what we see here therefore more or less represents the original design.

Somewhat remarkably the buildings have survived unaltered to the present day, save for the front of the canopy (left of the pillars) having been cut back recently.

Although two platforms, as seen here, were provided at the start, Maj.Gen. Hutchinson was told that it was intended to use the 'up' platform for all trains and was only willing to approve the

flat crossing for passengers to the other platform on that basis. In this view the flat crossing is still present, but later, after the 'down' platform came into regular use, the platforms were extended eastwards and passengers enabled to walk behind the stops instead of being in danger of a mowing down by a locomotive 'running round'.

(R. M. Casserley collection)

CHAPTER 6
The New Lines (1883-1893)

THE SOUTHEND-SHOEBURYNESS EXTENSION

In October 1882 the Board arranged the contract for this line with Kirk & Parry on the same 'schedule' as they were building the Sleaford-Spalding line for the GE & GN. Competitive tenders were not sought. In January it was noted that the works had commenced.

The extension was one of the most unexciting pieces of railway imaginable, the works comprising only some stretches of modest embankment and cutting of no note. The only real impact of the line was on Southend High Street, which it crossed by a bridge immediately beyond the station. (The line started directly from the stops of the existing terminus which became a through station as it stood). The intermediate country was almost empty, although this did not prevent a deputation waiting on Doughty Browne in June 1883 seeking an intermediate station, which was refused.

The line was inspected by Maj. Gen. Hutchinson in January 1884; his report of 21st January made no significant criticisms.

It opened on Friday 1st February 1884 without ceremony, although the first train, the 7.15am Southend-Shoeburyness, was reported 'largely patronised', as were most of the later trains that day. On Sunday 3rd 1200 tickets were sold to persons wishing to experience the new line. Goods traffic also began on 1st February.

In the first years the service was worked by Southend locos, hence the early morning Southend-Shoeburyness service to form the first up train. However a shed was built at Shoeburyness and opened at an unknown date in 1889/90, whereupon Southend shed was closed and its site used for the expansion of the station facilities.

THE BARKING-PITSEA LINE

It was decided to divide this line into two contracts, Barking-Upminster and Upminster-Pitsea. On 6th June 1883 the Board considered an offer by Kirk & Parry to build the line at the same prices as for the Shoeburyness extension, and this resulted in them being given the first contract on 20th July, again without any competitive tendering.

It was noted earlier that Stride was made 'Engineer' for the new lines at a supplemental fee above his normal salary as Manager. In this capacity it was for him to pay his staff out of his 'Engineer's fees'; accordingly in January 1884 when J.R. Robertson was appointed Resident Engineer for the line he was transferred from the LT&SR payroll to Stride's staff. The Engineer's office was set up at Hornchurch.

On Thursday 11th October 1883 a sod-cutting ceremony was held by Upminster windmill (seemingly the only time that such an event was ever staged on the LT&SR). A special train left Fenchurch Street at noon taking guests to Rainham where they transferred to seven 4-horse coaches for the short trip to Upminster. 'Here the leading gentry of the neighbourhood and the villagers gave the party a hearty welcome, and accompanied the guests to the favoured spot'. The Rev. Clementi Smith gave a blessing and Mrs Doughty Browne was presented with a spade to turn the first sod. Afterwards there was lunch in a marquee; Doughty Browne expressed the LT&SR's hopes for residential development in the area, and Stride spoke of 'keeping out jerry-builders'. (The latter aim was largely achieved; unfortunately it was to be many years before any development of note occurred at all!).

At Barking it had been intended originally to have the junction

Railway Station, Shoeburyness. 13.

A.H.Judd&Co
Southend-on-Sea.

61

The Station, Hornchurch.

HORNCHURCH

Thanks to the slow development of the area in the years after the line opened, Hornchurch station remained unchanged between opening in 1885 and the quadrupling of 1930/31. The goods yard was commodious enough for all likely needs of the period. The OS extract below, with the station still in the fields, is the 1915 survey; the 1894 survey is identical save for the fact that it shows a short ballast (?) siding on the up side which had gone by 1915 with the pit area being given over to a Rifle Range. The main station building, with stationmaster's house attached, was at street level, set back in a forecourt. The goods yard headshunt running off the left hand edge of the extract was also available as a Down Refuge Siding.

The view at lower left, taken from the signal box window, shows all the passenger facilities. It has also captured that rare thing a double-headed LT&SR train. The LT&SR did not engage in double-heading (except that a second loco that would otherwise have had to run light engine was sometimes attached to a train between Shoeburyness and Southend, to save line capacity). The heaviest trains took up the full length of Platform 4 at Fenchurch Street and there was no room for a second loco there. The reason why No.8 has been attached to this train can only be guessed at. It is about 5pm on a spring afternoon in the Edwardian years; the train is a heavy one (unless it is a Sunday, it will be working back as a down peak service) but should be within the capacity of the train engine.

The upper left view shows the station buildings at closer range. The stations on the new lines were built in this standard style, which will be

discussed further in an Appendix on LT&SR Architecture in Vol.2. Hornchurch was unusual in having lengthy canopies and a range of buildings on both platforms which shows the high expectations that had been held for a residential traffic here; most of the new lines stations only got a waiting room and short canopy on the 'other' platform.

The first Hornchurch signal box (right) opened with the line in 1885 and was abolished on 7th December 1930 when a new LMS design box opened. It was built by Easterbrook who, as noted in the text, did the signalling between Barking East Junction and East Horndon inclusive. The 25-lever Easterbrook frame remained in use until the box closed and was one of the last remaining on the LT&S line by then. Signalman Boswell is seen here in the early 1920s.
(Courtesy Bob Boswell)

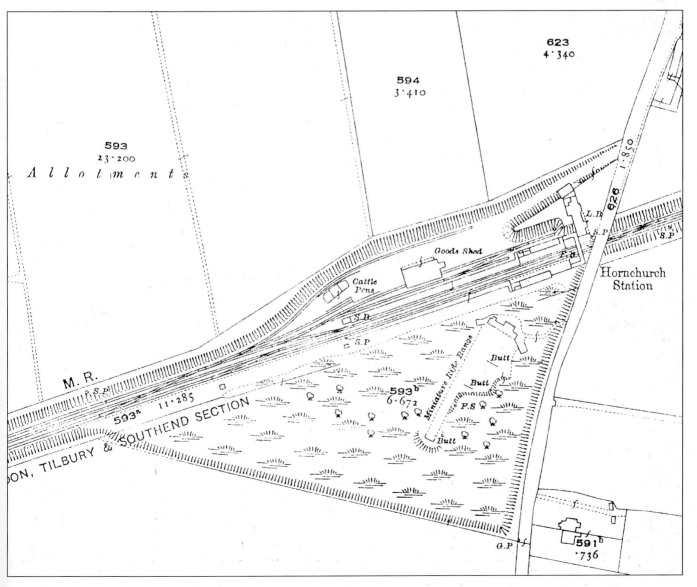

for the new line west of the station at Queens Road, so that Barking would have become a four-platform station like the new Pitsea. This was in connection with a proposed road bridge at East Street in lieu of the level crossing, which however fell through due to disagreement between the LT&SR and the Local Authority. It was then decided to move the junction to the east of East Street, to avoid the need for a second level crossing (for which powers would certainly not have been granted even if sought). This could be done within the existing 'limits of deviation'.

The seven and three-quarter miles of Contract No 1 (Barking to Upminster) were a relatively easy job and took only 18 months. In the cuttings at Dagenham and Hornchurch good gravel was found, and used to make concrete for the bridges instead of building them of brick (they were however faced with brick). The most notable structure was the 70-ft span girder underbridge over the Hornchurch-Upminster road (site of the later Upminster Bridge station). There were three stations, Dagenham, Hornchurch and Upminster; no doubts seem to have arisen in choosing the station sites, although Hornchurch was a bad half-mile from the nearest end of the village, unavoidably. Signalling work was let to Easterbrook Hannaford & Co in June 1884, on their offering to do it for 7½% less than their schedule prices; there were four boxes (Barking East Junction, and the three new stations).

The line to Upminster was opened for passenger and goods traffic on 1st May 1885, the very day that had been specified for completion in the contract, Maj. Gen. Hutchinson's inspection in April having produced no comments of significance. The station buildings were not all fully completed at opening. In the now-established LT&SR tradition there was no opening ceremony, although Mr Chalk the Barking stationmaster displayed flags and a motto 'Success to the New Line' on the footbridge, and Mr Stevens the new Dagenham stationmaster also ventured a display of flags. The Directors made a tour of the line on 14th

May and were entertained to lunch by Mr H. Joslin of Games Park, Upminster.

Contract No 2 (Upminster-Pitsea) was a much harder job owing to the territory between East Horndon and Pitsea. In October 1884 Kirk & Parry advised that they would like to begin work on this second section, and they were given the contract on 23rd October, again without competitive tendering. Work began early in 1885. A lengthy account of the works on this section was written in 1891 by Henry E. Stilgoe, one of the engineering staff, and enables us to give some details.

From Upminster to East Horndon the country was level, the biggest works being the long approach embankments for the roads over the five public road overbridges (level crossings were now definitely not desired). The railway could not be put in cutting to reduce these embankments, as the water level was only a few feet beneath the surface. These bridges were built of brick, as there was no convenient gravel on this section. East Horndon station was in an exceedingly remote position, but was compulsory under the 1882 Act as a sop to Lord Petre. The line from Upminster to East Horndon was opened (passenger and goods) on 1st May 1886, the Board of Trade inspection again producing no comments. This opening was more for show than in any likelihood of significant traffic being gained!

From East Horndon the line climbed for three and a half miles to the summit at Laindon, with heavy earthworks. Particular problems were encountered with the embankment at Dunton, which had a maximum height of 37ft. The ground was unstable clay and the embankment kept sinking whilst the fields either side 'bulged out like great waves, rising 12 or 15 feet above the original surface'. The men would sometimes come back in the morning to find that the bank had sunk 5ft overnight. Through this embankment was the Dunton road underbridge (or tunnel).

Immediately beyond was the 82-chain Laindon cutting, greatest depth 37ft, which was commenced on 30th June 1885 and completed on 28th April 1887. The 'cut' was used to make the

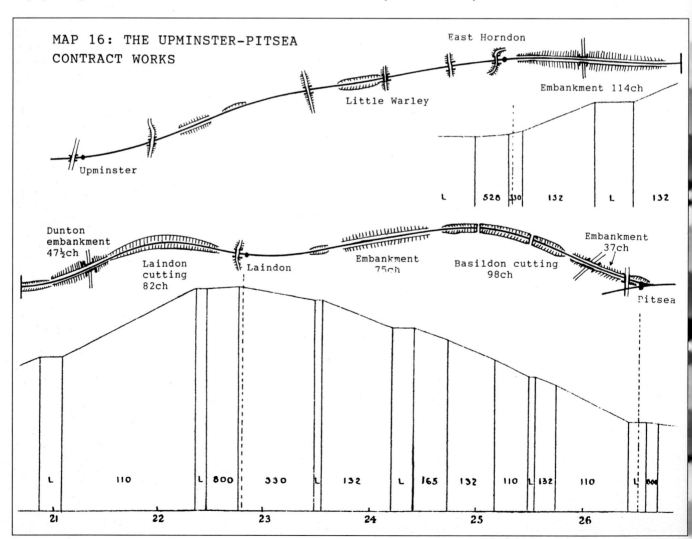

MAP 16: THE UPMINSTER-PITSEA CONTRACT WORKS

Dunton embankment. Two 'steam navvies' were used and at the height of the work were excavating 7486 cu yds per week, this forming 3327 tip wagon loads.

Further east there was another heavy cutting at Basildon, 98 chains in length and 30ft maximum depth. A Ruston & Proctor steam navvy was used here. Work began 7.5.1885 and ended 16.9.1887. Initially the 'cut' was used for the 75ch Laindon embankment immediately to the west, but, when this was completed, the remainder was taken to complete the embankment at East Horndon. This was a six-mile journey and had to be done in two portions with a rest at Laindon where a gang of boys were stationed to grease the axleboxes of the contractor's tip wagons, which were not designed for such lengthy trips. By 1887 the permanent way was laid for most of this distance and the trains could therefore be 'run at a good speed'. Stilgoe claimed that there was 'not a single wagon disabled through running hot'.

The final major work was the cutting at the west end of the new Pitsea station. Although only 28ch long with a maximum depth of 21ft, it was regarded as 'perhaps the most serious engineering question on the whole work', for the hill behind, on which Pitsea church stood, was 'cracking and sliding in all directions', as was all too evident in the church's condition. It was decided to build a strong retaining wall for 126 yds on the down side to hold back the hill.

At Pitsea an entirely new station was built with four platforms, to replace the original station at the level crossing a little way down the Tilbury line (although the original goods facilities were retained).

The Barking-Pitsea line in total involved 1,550,000 cu yds of excavation and the construction of 53 bridges. The contractors employed three steam navvies as mentioned, eight locomotives, 400 tip wagons, and 500-600 men. A 4' 8½" gauge 'Overland Route' was laid for the whole length of the line just outside the railway boundary for the transport of materials (this was now becoming an established practice amongst contractors, whereas in earlier days horse and cart on public roads had been the norm). The country was so empty that very few men were able to find lodgings near the line, and a train of trucks, known as 'The Mail', had to be run to bring men in daily from the London direction, using the 'Overland Route'. The contractors also built some cottages and stables at Dunton. There was a great shortage of water throughout the line, and this had to be brought in by rail.

The East Horndon-Pitsea section was opened for passenger and goods traffic on 1st June 1888 (Maj. Gen. Hutchinson having again found nothing to criticise). A modest private celebration was engaged in by the LT&SR officers who went down to Southend on the 6.30am from Fenchurch Street, breakfasted at the London Hotel, and returned on the 9.10am 'express', 'christening' the new line with a bottle of champagne at Pitsea. On 3rd June the Directors made an 'inspection' and lunched at Southend. The *Southend Standard* on 31st May had noted that 'there will be no flags in Southend tomorrow' but that it would be an important day for the town nevertheless.

The Dunton embankment soon brought trouble. On 2nd August 1888 there was a fearsome storm in South Essex with 5in of rain in a few hours, and what the LT&SR minutes referred to as a 'supposed water spout' destroyed much of this embankment. As a result the line was closed between East Horndon and Laindon until 1st October. For six days after 2nd August the Tilbury line was also closed by flooding and no trains could be run to Southend at all; £7,000 revenue was lost as a result, the Bank Holiday traffic being wiped out. From 8th August the pre-June 1st timetable was reverted to (plus a Laindon-Pitsea shuttle), until 1st October. The Dunton embankment suffered another subsidence, less seriously, in March 1910, and has remained a problem since.

ROMFORD-GRAYS

Nothing was done about this line for several years, partly because the LT&SR was preoccupied with the Barking-Pitsea line, and partly because there were vague hopes of some unexpected change of circumstances which might render it unnecessary to build the line at all. The 1883 Act powers expired in 1888, and were extended to 1889 by the LT&SR Act 1886 and then to 1891 by the LT&SR Act 1888. These extensions had of course to be approved by shareholders' meetings, an embarrassment for the Board. At the January 1886 meeting, Doughty Browne stated that it was not intended to postpone work on the line sine die, but it was considered prudent to see how the Tilbury docks traffic developed first. When the docks traffic turned out much poorer than expected, it naturally added grist to the mill of the 'antis'. After several years of meetings dominated by self-congratulation, the two 1888 shareholders' meetings saw harsh words spoken as a result. In January T. Adams (the Auditor) complained that he 'would like to see the line obliterated from the map, for he did not believe it would more than pay its working expenses'. Doughty Browne could only respond that abandonment 'would leave our flank open to a competing line'. In July a Captain Pavy made many complaints; Doughty Browne replied 'Much as I regret having to spend this additional capital to make this line, I think it would be better to make it than to let it go', and was relieved to hear cries of 'Hear! Hear!' from the floor.

Playing on this unease, Birt, the GER General Manager, informally suggested to Doughty Browne in April 1888 that the GER might build part of the line instead. This was not pursued, but in September Birt proposed that if the LT&SR built the Romford-Upminster section the GER would lease it at a rental of 3% on the outlay provided that they were given running powers to Tilbury by this route (ie via Ockendon, the Upminster-Grays section being built as a normal LT&SR line). This idea was seriously considered by the LT&SR Board, but rejected in October.

By this date Stride had prepared the contract plans for Upminster-Grays and was about to go on to those for Romford-Upminster. The whole line was now to be built single (in 1883 it had all been intended as double). The inevitable was now faced up to, and in November 1888 the solicitors were instructed to serve land notices for the whole line. On 4th July 1889 the Board considered tenders for the Upminster-Grays section, and accepted that of Mowlem - who did most of the larger LT&SR jobs from this time on - which was the lowest at £46,560. Kirk & Parry and Lucas & Aird were among the rejected tenders. Work began on this section soon afterwards. J. R. Robertson was again Resident Engineer, the office remaining at Hornchurch; George Burt was Mowlem's engineer on the works.

The largest work on this section was the 14-arch brick viaduct over the Mar Dyke at Stifford. (This had been shown as an embankment on the plans in 1883. It was the only viaduct on the LT&SR apart from the section between Gas Factory Junction and Campbell Road Junction). It had a maximum height of 32'9" and was built for double track, as (in the normal way) were the overbridges and some of the other underbridges; land was also taken for double track. Around June 1890 the new junction and signal box at 'West Thurrock Junction' west of Grays were brought into use for the contractor's convenience, the box also controlling a siding leading into Mowlem's 'Overland Route'.

The only station was at Ockendon, which was made a passing place. There was also a public siding, 'North Ockendon Agricultural Siding', between Upminster and Ockendon. The brochure produced for the October 1883 sod-cutting ceremony at Upminster had shown further stations on the branch at Stifford and West Thurrock; Stride had also specifically stated in parliament in 1883 that there would be a station at West Thurrock, and it might be noted also that two of the LT&SR's new locomotives - which were all named after stations - in 1884 were named *Stifford* and *West Thurrock*. By 1889 however economy was the prime consideration.

The Upminster-West Thurrock Junction section was inspected by Maj. Gen. Hutchinson on 26th June 1892, and he being once again quite content with all, was opened for passenger and goods traffic on 1st July 1892.

The contract for the Romford-Upminster section was given to Mowlem, on the same 'schedule', in June 1890. Work was under way by the end of the year at the Upminster end, but at this stage it was still not fixed what the station arrangements at Romford would be. The 1883 Act had authorised a junction half

To page 69

PITSEA

left
The first Pitsea station, seen in the OS 25" plan of c1865. When the 200ft platforms seen here were extended eastwards to 510ft in 1881, the eastern connection from the down line to the goods yard had to be removed. Also in 1881 the goods shed was extended.

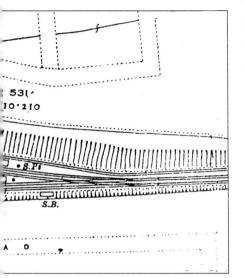

above
The second station, in the 1915 25" plan. There had been no changes since the station opened in 1888 (save that the siding at far left was an addition of the 1900s). It is believed that this station opened and the first station closed on 1st June 1888 when the new line opened, but no specific statement of the exact date is known. The far

western ends of the 1888 station's Tilbury line platforms actually 'overlapped' by a short distance the eastern ends of the first station's platforms as extended. Comparison with the earlier map shows how the goods facilities remained on much the same site in 1888, although almost all the trackwork of the goods yard was actually new. The sidings behind the up and down Upminster line platforms were probably meant primarily for empty coaching stock, as many trains terminated at Pitsea in the LT&SR period. Note the speculators' streets laid out either side of the station, sans houses; they never did get many houses built! The level crossing on the Tilbury line, latterly known as 'Pitsea Hall Crossing', still remains. The goods yard was taken out in October 1967.

middle left
Pitsea, looking east from the road bridge over the Upminster line in the 1900s. The main station buildings were at street level in the fork, with footbridges leading in both directions. The standard LT&SR station architecture of the 1880s is discussed in an Appendix in Vol. 2. At left is the retaining wall built to hold back the unstable hillside which caused the engineers so much concern.
(Paul Armstrong collection)

lower left
In 1934 the siding behind the up Upminster line platform was converted to a passenger bay line, as seen here in this late 1930s view from the Upminster line footbridge. Note the 'Pitsea Junction' nameboard - the station was never so called in timetables or any other official source. The small additional board below cannot be read but it may be 'For Vange', as the station's official name was 'Pitsea for Vange' from 1932 to 1953. It then reverted to plain 'Pitsea' and was so on the

new ER 1950s nameboards, but the boards soon had 'Alight Here for Basildon' added in celebration of the inconveniently-rail-served New Town.

All the 1888 platform waiting shelters and canopies are seen here. In the distance is the LMS signal box also of 1934. This was built because a new engine spur line provided in 1934 at the east end of the Tilbury line platforms, to enable locos to run round a train from Tilbury terminating here without fouling the main line, ran through the site of the 1888 box. The 1934 box was itself replaced by a new panel box in 1960.

In late 1956 the Upminster line platforms were extended for 12 car trains and the bay platform was removed. Soon afterwards the 1888 main station buildings at street level were removed and a new BR building erected on their site. The only 1888 structures extant in 1994 are the Upminster line footbridge (now coverless) and the down Upminster platform waiting shelter.
(R. C. Riley collection)

below
A fine atmospheric view from the east end of the platforms in the late summer sunshine of Sunday 26th September 1948. 41967 (LT&SR No 81) still with 'LMS' on the tank, awaits departure with a down main line train. The corrugated-arm signals would date from 1934. The 1934 Engine Spur referred to above is seen at right.
(A. G. Ellis collection)

LONDON, BARKING, TILBURY, GRAVESEND, SOUTHEND.—London, Tilbury, and Southend.

Bradshaw, July 1883. The Barking 'shorts' now comprise the majority of LT&SR trains. Note that four of them (7.35, 3.23, 5.22, 7.15 down; 8.43, 4.15, 6.17 and 7.55 up) are extended to Rainham - this Rainham service lasted into the '90s. The last train from Fenchurch Street at night is now as late as 12 midnight to Barking and this train was extended to Tilbury a few years later. (At one time the last train had been early as 8.40pm but this had been improved on by stages in the 1870s). Note also the two early morning up trains at 5.10am and 6.10am from Barking, which had been added around 1880. The basic service of 8 trains to Southend and 14 to Tilbury is only slightly above 1860s levels.

The main 'residential' trains here are the 8.55 up from Tilbury (actually through from Southend) for Gravesend traffic, and the 9.0am up from Southend non-stop, with corresponding down services at 5.5pm to Southend and 5.15pm to Tilbury. For details of the development of these services see Chapter 9.

The Liverpool Street-Barking service is still only 4 trains, this being just before the introduction of the enhanced service.

Note the Chalk Farm-Southend through trains on Sundays and Mondays, and the daily Margate Boat Trains (with through coaches from Chalk Farm) now running to Tilbury instead of Thames Haven.

The main ferry service ran from Gravesend West Street Pier at this period (1880-5), following disagreement with Gravesend Corporation over the use of the Town Pier. However in 1885 the LT&SR bought the Town Pier, and transferred the passenger boats back there, where they remained until 1965.

68

a mile east of Romford with LT&SR running powers into the GER station. However the GER now, not unreasonably, objected to their line capacity being reduced in this way. Negotiations between Stride and the GER showed little sign of success, and by summer 1891 it was suspected that the matter would have to be taken to arbitration. Eventually, however, an agreement (the formal document was dated 20.3.1893) was reached in April 1892, on the basis

- The LT&SR to build an independent line into Romford beside the GER line, and their own station at Romford, the latter to be on GER land for which £100pa would be paid in rent

- The 1883 Act junction to be given up, but a junction to be made immediately east of the GER station for use by LT&SR goods trains.

- The GER to provide facilities for LT&SR goods traffic at their Romford goods station (which was west of the passenger station) for at least the first three years, after which either company could raise the question of separate goods accommodation for the LT&SR being necessary.

The whole section had quite heavy earthworks, being against the lie of the land. The major work however was the building of a 1260ft-long retaining wall at Romford along the south side of the GER property, the space behind which was then infilled to make the ground for the LT&SR station. This wall was begun on 6th December 1892 and completed on 30th April 1893, using 1¹/₂ million bricks.

After inspection by Hutchinson on 5th June, the Romford-Upminster section was opened on Wednesday 7th June 1893. As ever there was no ceremony. The LT&SR Board had rejected applications for a station at Butts Green for the benefit of Hornchurch people going to Romford (but this was to resurface after the Emerson Park Estate was built - see later). The question of train services was discussed by the Board on 15.5.1893; they decided that 'the present prospects of traffic would only justify a small service', and left Stride to arrange it in detail.

PASSENGER TRAIN SERVICES 1875-1894
On the takeover of the line in July 1875, the train service was re-examined and changes made for 'greater convenience'. These however were largely minor; and indeed the late '70s and early '80s saw little enhancement of the basic services to Tilbury and Southend, there being still no demand to justify anything much beyond the original level of service. The most marked change of these years was the growth in the number of Fenchurch Street-Barking 'shorts', from 6 in 1875 (no increase on 1862) to 21 in the 1883 timetable here, as the suburban areas developed. Barking itself was little developed as yet, but was the natural terminus for these services. (After 1885, with two routes to serve beyond, the number of trains terminating at Barking was much reduced even though the total number of trains increased. However a platform for terminating trains was provided in the enlarged Barking station of 1889). Passengers benefited in the late '70s from the provision of an entirely new carriage fleet in place of the use of old GER stock.

Opening to Shoeburyness (1884). Almost all Fenchurch Street-Southend trains were extended to Shoeburyness, and this continued to be the practice subsequently. Also, a few Leigh-Southend-Shoeburyness 'shorts' were put on to fill gaps in the main service; these continued in most (not all) subsequent timetables.

Opening to Upminster (1885). When the line opened to Upminster on 1.7.1885 a good service of 16 trains each way was provided, all calling at Dagenham and Hornchurch. This was done by extending to Upminster most of the trains which had previously terminated at Barking. However the Chairman was obliged to note in July 1886 that this rather speculative service level had not produced much traffic, and it was reduced in October 1886.

Opening to East Horndon (1886). Only a minimal 5 down/6 up trains were extended through to East Horndon from 1.7.1886.

Opening of the new through route via Laindon (1888). The expensively-built new route did not bring benefits to all LT&SR passengers. Those travelling between Fenchurch Street and stations Pitsea to Shoeburyness benefited most, but

even so only about half the Southend service was diverted via Laindon in the first years after 1888, the remaining trains continuing to run via Tilbury with no reduction in journey time. To supplement the few Southend trains on the Laindon route, other Fenchurch Street-Pitsea via Laindon services were provided, but many of these had poor or no connections at Pitsea for Southend, and one imagines that they ran pretty empty. There were now only a couple or so Fenchurch Street-Upminster 'shorts', so the total service to Upminster remained below the 1885 level.

As an illustration, the weekday down service on the Laindon route in the July 1889 timetable was (times from Fenchurch Street).

+6.45 am	Shoeburyness
8.23 am	Southend
8.57 am	Upminster
9.28 am	Shoeburyness (fast Barking - Upminster - Leigh)
10.28 am	Upminster
11.50 am	Pitsea (half hour wait for connection beyond)
2.15 pm	Pitsea (55 min. wait for connection beyond)
3.50 pm	Pitsea (no connection beyond)
4.52 pm	Upminster
5.05 pm	Shoeburyness express (non stop to Southend)
+5.53 pm	Shoeburyness
6.08 pm	Southend, fast Stepney - Hornchurch - Upminser - Leigh
7.15 pm	Pitsea (50 min. wait for connection beyond)
9.00 pm	Shoeburyness

+ These trains may have terminated at Pitsea with immediate connection to Southend; the situation is unclear in Bradshaw.

The continued running of many Shoeburyness trains via Tilbury initially did at least ensure the continuation of a reasonable service over the Tilbury-Southend leg. In the '90s, however, these trains were gradually diverted to run via Laindon instead, until only odd trains were still running through from London to Southend via Tilbury. The result was that the Tilbury-Southend service became exceedingly poor, with most Tilbury line trains terminating at Pitsea and connections there not particularly good. This was gradually improved in the 1900s when more Tilbury line trains were extended through to Shoeburyness again.

All this was effectively a reflection of the fact that in the years after 1888 there was simply not yet enough Southend traffic to justify two lines, and the result was a poor service on both lines! Of course the Laindon route was a necessity in the longer term, but in the short term it was something of a nuisance to the timetablers.

The LT&SR obtained powers to maintain fares to Pitsea and beyond at the existing level, despite the reduced mileage.

The enhanced London-Tilbury service (1886)
It will be recalled that the 1883 LT&SR/East & West India Dock Co agreement had required the LT&SR to provide an enhanced Fenchurch Street-Tilbury service from the opening of the docks. This service was duly introduced on 19th April 1886. There were now 24 trains per day to Tilbury instead of 15, with a half-hourly frequency in the middle of the day. The additional trains mostly called at Stepney, Plaistow (for the NLR connection as specified in the agreement), Grays, Tilbury Dock(s), and Tilbury only. The 'not more than 40 minutes' journey time to Tilbury Dock(s) station was not quite achieved, 41 minutes being the norm.

There was of course never the traffic to justify this level of service. In January 1889 Stride wrote to the Dock Co to say that the service would have to be curtailed. They would not make up a guarantee of 2s 6d per train mile, and accordingly 5 down and 4 up trains were taken off from 1st April 1889. This still left a better service than pre-1886 and it remained so subsequently.

Workmen's tickets.
By s.50 of the LT&SR Act 1882, powers were obtained to run Workmen's trains at fares not exceeding ¹/₄d per mile.

Workmen's tickets were then introduced (by 1885) from stations Barking to Bromley to Fenchurch Street, available up by the 5.10, 6.10 and 7.0am trains from Barking, returning by any train after 4pm (12 noon on Saturdays).

This was a small start to what was to become a much larger traffic. In 1893, by which date there were five permitted up trains and no restrictions on the time of the return journey, the fares were reduced to 3d return from Barking and East Ham, 2 1/2d from Upton Park, and 2d from Plaistow and Bromley. The tickets could be bought in packets of six for the week (although no further reduction was obtained by this). By 1903 there were 11 early morning trains designated as 'Workmen's', the first the 4.40am from Barking and the last the 7.26am. There were also Workmen's fares on the St Pancras-East Ham service.

Burdett Road stops.
Under the LT&SR Act 1891, the LT&SR were empowered for the first time to stop trains at all stations between Gas Factory Junction and Fenchurch Street. (Previously the LT&SR trains had only called at Stepney, except that occasionally stops had been made at the other stations for school excursion parties). As a result, LT&SR trains began calling at Burdett Road on 1st November 1891. As a quid pro quo, the GER were entitled to stop their North Woolwich trains at Bromley from the same date (they were not allowed this under the 1876 agreement, although they had in fact been allowed to call at Bromley previously in 1883-7, until Stride had the arrangement withdrawn on line capacity grounds, which problem had now to be forgotten). 'LT&S' calls at Burdett Road continued until the station closed in 1941.

Although the 1891 Act also gave power to stop at Shadwell and Leman Street, it was not actually planned to stop LT&SR trains at these stations, and they never did. These two stations only had platforms on the southern pair of lines.

GER COMPETITION TO SOUTHEND
The new GER route to Southend was opened on 1st October 1889, but did not bring an immediate full GER attack on Southend. The line was single between Wickford and Southend (doubling was only completed in 1901). The initial service was only 6 trains each way, all except one involving a change at Shenfield. For summer 1890 there were 12, of which 6 were through; for the following winter 8, of which 3 were through. It abstracted some traffic from the LT&SR, all the same, and affected revenues. The LT&SR rebuilt its Southend station in 1889 to provide better passenger facilities; this had been under consideration since 1885 but was only authorised, at an estimate of £20,000, in 1888.

The LT&SR's fears of passengers being attracted away from Fenchurch Street to the more convenient Liverpool Street now resurfaced, and in May 1890 Stride drew up (with some nerve!) plans for a service of LT&SR trains from Liverpool Street to Southend as from 1st June, to supplant the existing badly-patronised through coaches on the GER Liverpool Street-Barking trains (see Chapter 5 for this service). Birt not surprisingly objected on the grounds that the LT&SR had no running powers into Liverpool Street - and the trains had to be deleted from the draft timetable.

In August 1890 the GER campaign on Southend traffic was stepped up, with the introduction of through excursion trains from Fenchurch Street to Southend GE. The Booking Clerks at Fenchurch Street were GER employees and could be instructed to influence traffic to the GER trains, so in October Stride suggested that the LT&SR should, for the first time, appoint its own clerks there (which they were entitled to do under the 1876 agreement). Another, more underhand, act by the GER was seen on August Bank Holiday Monday when they suspended the Liverpool Street-Barking service for much of the day, so rendering it impossible for people to go to Southend via the LT&SR! - the GER claimed this was all due to a mistake by an Inspector, but they were not believed.

The LT&SR responded by seeking running powers to Liverpool Street in its 1891 Bill (it will be recalled that this had been previously attempted, in vain, in 1883). Powers were only sought for up to 8 trains a day, so that the GER could not claim

line capacity problems, the idea being that the existing GER Barking trains would be replaced by a new LT&SR Liverpool Street-Southend service. The GER naturally opposed this clause in parliament, and succeeded in getting the Commons Committee to throw it out. The only sop granted to the LT&SR was that the GER should henceforth charge the same fare from Liverpool Street to Southend LT&S as to Southend GE (they had previously been charging 2d more by the LT&S route).

The GER attack resumed in summer 1891 with the introduction in July of a 65-minute GER residential express (8.45am from Southend, 5.25pm from Liverpool Street). In March 1891 it had been stated by Birt that the GER had only one Southend season-ticket holder, so there was certainly scope for attracting more of this traffic. The timing was cut to 60 minutes in October.

The 'third wave' came in June 1892 when the GER put on two timetabled daily through trains from Fenchurch Street to Southend GE (9.47am and 10.47am from Fenchurch Street, and 6.48pm and 8.38pm from Southend), in an attempt to extract daytripper traffic from the LT&SR's maws. The GER Southend line timetable (which up to now had not shown Fenchurch Street at all) was rearranged to make it look as though there were many trains from Fenchurch Street to Southend GE, when in reality all but these two were existing trains involving a change at Stratford for Southend! The LT&SR did now appoint their own booking clerks at Fenchurch Street; they also improved their Southend service, and had the Liverpool Street-Barking service brought back to 8 trains each way. At the February 1893 LT&SR shareholders' meeting, Doughty Browne made a rather exaggerated report on this GER Southend competition, claiming that the GER had been running twelve trains from Fenchurch Street to Southend GE the previous summer. Somewhat surprisingly the two actual GER trains from Fenchurch Street continued to run in the winter timetables also. (They were still running in the 1900s).

The opening of the GER line to Southend also brought the end of second class coaches on the LT&SR. In January 1893 the GER withdrew 2nd class facilities from all trains except those in the inner suburban area, and began issuing 3rd class seasons to Southend. (At this period 3rd class passengers were not generally allowed season tickets, except where 2nd class was abolished). The LT&SR saw this as a threat to their Southend residential traffic, which was primarily 2nd class (although 2nd class was of little significance by this date in the LT&SR's traffic at large) with over 500 2nd class Southend season ticket holders. Accordingly the Board resolved to withdraw 2nd class facilities on the LT&SR also, which was done as from 1.1.1893 for stations east of Pitsea, and as from 1.4.1893 for the rest of the system. At the July shareholders' meeting it was presented as another piece of GER aggression that would cost the LT&SR dearly. But 2nd class was a fading thing nationally, and the LT&SR themselves had considered abolishing it in 1890 before the GER had done anything. Indeed, they had sought powers for this in their 1891 Bill (unsuccessfully - but there was no absolute need for specific powers anyway).

The abstraction of Southend traffic did damage the LT&SR. In 1890 the LT&SR's revenue decreased for the first time in many years, and the dividend (which had already been falling yearly from the 6% high of the early '80s, as a result of the new lines greatly increasing the capital without bringing in much extra revenue) sunk to an all-time low of 3 1/2%. For a time LT&SR stock sank below par on the market. Having reduced the LT&SR to such a state, this was the very time when the GER should have stepped in and made a takeover offer; but they did not move. They never had such a good chance again, as the LT&SR's finances improved again gradually through the '90s, with population increases bringing extra traffic to reward the company's 1880s investments.

THE LT&SR AND FENCHURCH STREET AND THE LONDON & BLACKWALL LINE
It was recounted in Chapter 2 how the L&BR had enlarged Fenchurch Street station to four platforms in 1853/4 and then brought into use a third line for up trains (on the north side) between Stepney Junction and Fenchurch Street in 1856. By

these means LT&SR (and ECR and NLR) trains were accommodated satisfactorily for many years. The LT&SR trains were but a small fraction of the station's traffic in these early years.

In 1869 the GER improved the working by bringing the Block System into use between Fenchurch Street and Gas Factory Junction and Bow Junction in place of time-interval working, and providing interlocked signal boxes at all locations on the L&B line. (The running of the service on foggy days pre-1869 does not bear thinking about too closely!).

When the GER took over the L&BR in 1866 they investigated the possibility of using Fenchurch Street for more GE suburban services (only the North Woolwich trains, and Loughton branch trains, were currently using it). However they concluded that there was insufficient capacity for further services to be run there. But eventually services from Fenchurch Street to Forest Gate and Lower Edmonton were introduced in 1877.

This, and the increasing number of LT&SR trains, meant that the 1850s arrangements could no longer cope. In 1882 the whole layout was remodelled, a fifth platform added on the north side, and the other platforms lengthened, including the extension of Platform 4 (to the 765ft form in which it lasted until the 1935 remodelling) for the use of LT&SR trains, many of which were now of considerable length. The station buildings and overall roof were not altered, but the formation was much widened on the north side at the Minories end to accommodate the 'new' Platform 4 and additional Platform 5. The works were inspected by Maj. Gen. Hutchinson in January 1883. It was in connection with this remodelling that the gantried signal box that lasted until 1935 was built.

After this, Platform 4 was given over to the LT&SR's use (although a very few LT&SR trains used Platform 3, and ran over the southernmost up line from Stepney Junction in the up direction instead of the 'third line'). However this was purely an agreed matter; there was never anything in the agreements (of 1876 and later) regarding the LT&SR's use of the station that restricted LT&SR trains to any particular platform or the use of any particular tracks on the L&B line.

In 1881 a new office block was built by the GER for the LT&SR's use abutting on to the north side of the station in John Street. This incorporated an additional Booking Office with a subway leading to Platforms 4 & 5 (only), and was much used as an entrance by LT&SR passengers, relieving the main concourse area.

By 1885 there were five LT&SR trains leaving Fenchurch Street in the evening peak hour, compared with three in the 1870s (5.5 Shoeburyness 'express', 5.15 Tilbury fast, 5.22 Rainham, 5.45 Shoeburyness, 5.53 Upminster). This was as much as could be accommodated at the terminus and in 1900 there were still only these five trains in the same period. Turnrounds of five or six minutes meant that punctual running of inwards services was vital. This aspect is dealt with further in Chapter 9.

The proposed running of many extra Tilbury trains in connection with the docks made the GER concerned over line capacity (the L&BR line was carrying a considerable goods traffic at 'off-peak' times to the many goods depots between Stepney and Fenchurch Street, in addition to the increased passenger traffic). As a result it was provided in s.33 of the LT&SR Act 1882 that the LT&SR should pay a sum, to be settled by arbitration, to the costs of providing a fourth line if required between Fenchurch Street and Stepney. In 1884 the GER and LT&SR agreed that the fourth line (for down trains) was needed, and the powers were obtained in the L&BR Act 1885. The Bill had actually included a clause requiring the LT&SR to pay the whole cost of the fourth line! - but the LT&SR petitioned against this, and a section was added in the Act obliging the arbitrator to take account of benefits to GER services also. This question was to drag on for 18 years, until 1902. In 1886 John Walker, the General Manager of the North British, was agreed as arbitrator, but he died before he could do anything. Then the initial failure of Tilbury Docks meant that the extra traffic anticipated therefrom did not materialise, enabling the widening to be put off. The powers were several times revived, and eventually work began and the fourth line was brought into use in 1896. From the north side the four lines were now Down Fast (the new line), Up Fast, Down Slow, Up Slow; all (with very few exceptions) LT&SR trains were now booked to use the Fast lines although a few still used Platform 3 instead of 4. The c1895 OS maps in Hawkins, *Great Eastern in Town and Country Vol 1*, Irwell Press, show the widening in process with many sections of unconnected track; the viaduct was actually widened on the *south* side for the first 600 yards west of Stepney and all the lines slewed southwards over that stretch. The new Down Fast in fact began just outside Fenchurch Street as the turntable prevented a fourth line into the platforms; this naturally was an operating hindrance and in 1905 there were LT&SR/GER negotiations about removing the turntable to increase capacity, but this did not come to pass.

On completion of the widening the GER sought agreement on a new arbitrator but the LT&SR insisted on taking the case to

FENCHURCH STREET TRAIN SERVICES

The figures given are the number of down trains leaving the station on Mondays to Fridays. Seasonal differences were never significant (a few extra LT&SR trains ran in the summer at off-peak times).

	JUNE 1855	JULY 1875	JAN 1892	AUG 1913
L&BR/GER Blackwall line (1841-1926)	58	61	73	65
ECR/GER North Woolwich line (1854-1940)				
via Stratford	27	19	28	34
via Bromley	—	14	21	19
ECR/GER Loughton line (1856-1947)	—	22	24	25
GER Colchester line (1877-1949)	—	—	18	42
NLR/GER via/to Bow NLR (1859-1892)	58	60	30	—
LT&SR (1854-)	11	19	40	59
Total	154	195	234	244
LT&SR as percentage	7%	10%	17%	24%

Note - Gallions trains (from 1881) included under North Woolwich
    - Colchester line trains mostly to Forest Gate or Ilford
    -There were also shortlived services to Edmonton Low Level (commenced 1877) and Palace Gates (1880)
    -The ending of the Bow service in 1892 did not reduce the total number of trains as the paths were used for extra trains to Stratford and Forest Gate.

the Railway Commissioners instead. They considered the case in May 1897 and gave judgement in principle, but reserved certain matters to the report of Sir Benjamin Baker, who reported in May 1898 enabling the Commissioners to make their full judgement in December. However the LT&SR remained dissatisfied and went to the court of Appeal which heard the case in December 1900. The matter soured LT&SR/GER relationships in the 1896-1901 period but agreement was eventually reached in January 1902 after discussions between Stride and Gooday the GER General Manager. In March 1902 the LT&SR paid £17,000 representing the interest due on their share of the cost, and at the July LT&SR shareholders' meeting it was reported that 'all differences with the Great Eastern company arising out of the widening of the London & Blackwall Railway have been amicably settled, and the relations between the companies are of the most friendly character'.

By the 1890s the LT&SR services, whilst still only about 20% of the total number of trains, had become much the most important of the five Fenchurch Street services (LT&SR, Blackwall, Loughton, Ilford, and North Woolwich/Gallions) in terms of passenger numbers. There was serious platform overcrowding on Platform 4 in the peak hours, as the alighting passengers fought their way through the crowd waiting on the platform to board the train. This situation grew steadily worse until the opening of the Whitechapel & Bow line in 1902 relieved the pressure somewhat.

Another matter that came up at this period was the rent to be paid by the LT&SR for the use of Fenchurch Street station. This (under the 1876 LT&SR/GER Agreement) had been £4,000 pa since 1877, but with increasing use being made the GER sought an increase in 1895. After twelve months' haggling, agreement was reached in March 1896 on increased rents for the period 1895-1905, as set out in the table here. (A further agreement was then made in 1906 covering the next ten years, again as tabulated here).

The rent paid for the use of the L&B line between Gas Factory Junction and Fenchurch Street did not cause any problems in this way as, being based on traffic levels, it was increasing year by year. By 1900/01 the payment was up to £52,738 plus a further £10,138 for goods traffic. However the GER then became concerned over the possible loss of revenue if much of

RENT PAID BY LT&SR FOR USE OF FENCHURCH STREET STATION

from	July	1875	£3,000pa	(1876 Agreement)
from	July	1877	£4,000pa	
from	July	1895	£6,000pa	(1896 Agreement)
from	July	1897	£6,500pa	
from	July	1899	£7,000pa	
from	July	1901	£7,500pa	
from	July	1903	£8,000pa	
from	July	1906	£8,500pa	(1906 Agreement)
from	July	1908	£9,000pa	
from	July	1910	£9,500pa	
from	July	1912	£10,000pa	
from	July	1914	£10,500pa	(1912 Agreement)

the LT&SR passenger traffic were diverted over the Whitechapel & Bow line instead. Gooday therefore instigated negotiations for a revised agreement, which was reached in January 1902. This provided for a minimum payment of £32,000 pa by the LT&SR (against only £4,000 pa minimum in the 1876 Agreement). Even if all LT&SR passenger services were withdrawn from the line, a minimum of £11,000 was to apply.

A formal Agreement dated 11.6.1902 covered both this and the question of payment for the widening of the L&B line.

This did not actually affect the payments made in the years immediately after 1902, as the figures remained above the minimum in the event, despite the diversion of some traffic to the District trains. However, after the District electrification in 1905, the diversion of inner LT&SR traffic away from Fenchurch Street became more marked, and from 1907 only the minimum £32,000 was paid. Nevertheless, the LT&SR was (with the Blackwall line declining) if anything even more dominant at Fenchurch Street by 1912.

The LT&SR dealt with milk, fish, meat and vegetables also at Fenchurch Street (by passenger train).